begin.

elizabeth maxon

Back Porch Press
CLEMSON, SOUTH CAROLINA

Back Porch Press
Clemson, SC USA
www.elizabethmaxon.com

All scripture quotations are from The Message translation, unless otherwise noted.
Peterson, Eugene H. *The Message: The Bible in Contemporary Language.* Colorado Springs: NavPress, 2002.

PRINTED IN THE UNITED STATES OF AMERICA
ISBN: 978-0-9987868-0-3
Library of Congress Control Number:

begin./Elizabeth Maxon – 1st ed.

For My Tuesday Girls

with whom begin. began,
these words are richer and deeper because of you.

Thank you for your willingness to 'go someplace else' with me.
#mytuesdaygirls

*A good journey starts with knowing where we are
and being willing to go someplace else.*
~ Richard Rohr, "Everything Belongs"

~ Contents ~

Note from the Author

I seek to speak to you, in some way, as your own self. Who can tell what this may mean? I myself do not know, but if you listen, things will be said that are perhaps not written in this book. And this will be due not to me but to the One who lives and speaks in both.
~ Thomas Merton, "The Seven Storey Mountain"

One of my best friends isn't really into reading. I give her a hard time, but...I get it.

Some people don't excitedly crack open a book as if it were a treasure chest. Some people don't sniff pages like a drug addict. Some people don't live by Beverly Cleary's D.E.A.R. motto {Drop Everything And READ!}. Some people don't even *know* who Beverly Clearly is {gasp!}. Some people don't let their children watch a marathon of movies so they can finish those last few chapters of a riveting novel.

If you're not a reader, that's ~~heartbreaking~~ ok. Instead of trying to turn you into a reader {as I have unsuccessfully done to my poor husband}, I am hoping I have written a book for readers and non-readers alike.

When I told my friend about 'begin.' her eyes lit up. She realized she might actually get a 'Cliff Notes' version of a topic important to her. Maybe she will, maybe she won't. But I do hope this book will serve a purpose for all of us. God wants us to be intentional in our pursuit of him – reader or non-reader.

You may have noticed there is no subtitle on the cover. That was by design. I forget a lot of things, but that wasn't one of them. The truth is, I was hesitant to tell you the specific topic too early for fear you would never pick this book up. I suppose I can't put it off any longer. This book is about {drumroll, please}...spiritual disciplines!

Wait! No! Don't you close this book! Don't you give up on me yet!

When my pastor asked me to preach a sermon on spiritual disciplines a few years ago, I thought it was a joke. Really. I laughed. First of all, I have never been to seminary. Surely something as serious and important as spiritual disciplines required a professional. I am no professional.

Secondly, bo-ring. Let's just be honest. I actually like to engage with people when I speak to them and telling them how to pray or study their Bible didn't seem like it would go over well. I imagined everyone falling asleep within the first five minutes.

But it was no joke, so I reluctantly agreed. What happened over the next month shocked me. As I read, studied, wrote, and steeped myself in this topic of spiritual disciplines, my world was rocked. My relationship with Jesus moved from grayscale to technicolor. I was so transformed that I could hardly wait to take the stage and passionately pour out all I had discovered. The staff at our church agreed it was the most powerful sermon I had ever preached. Who would have guessed!? I fell in love with spiritual disciplines and I have been inviting others into this love affair ever since.

So get that image of monotone monks praying in a monastery out of your head. Resist the urge to use worn-out words like 'devo' or 'quiet time'. Don't feel overwhelmed or underqualified. Give spiritual disciplines a chance and I bet they will give you room to breathe and space to soar. If it could happen to an ordinary, non-seminary grad girl like me, it could happen to you too.

There are many who have walked this road of spiritual disciplines ahead of me – Dallas Willard, Richard Foster, Ruth Haley Barton, and Brother Lawrence - just to name a few. They possess wisdom and experience beyond my own, so I encourage you to listen to their voices as well. They can provide you with a more comprehensive examination of the disciplines not found here.

This book is intended as a crash course, to give you the basics and then quickly get you weaving them into the fabric of your days. In my own life, more information often leads to less transformation.

This is simply a place to begin.

That is often the hardest part, isn't it?
Getting out of bed.
Getting dressed.
Taking the first step.
Seeking answers before you even know the questions.
So let's begin.

The practices you utilize to connect yourself closer to God will not look exactly like mine. We are all created differently and we will all experience God uniquely, but I will offer some suggestions to get us all headed in the right direction.

In addition to my {hopefully} non-bossy suggestions about the art of implementing spiritual disciplines, I am also including 40 readings to get you started. You will notice there is no particular theme for these readings other than they all pertain to the beauty and truth of the gospel.

The reason for this apparent randomness is twofold — first, it is my natural tendency to flit from one thing to another. This is why I write on a variety of subjects. This is why I have a dozen half-completed projects all over my house. I have undiagnosed ADHD and I am the self-proclaimed 'queen of random' so I want to be honest in saying - that's what you are going to get from me.

Secondly, the readings are intended to whet your appetite. I hope the variety will provide you with a chance to experiment with different topics and styles of writing to see what may best encourage your digging and growing in God's word.

ATTENTION: If at any point you begin to feel bogged down by the opening chapters, feel free to jump ahead to the daily readings. There will not be a test to determine what you read and retained. My feelings will not be hurt if you skip over something. It is MOST important to me that you ultimately gain a greater awareness of God's presence and begin living out spiritual disciplines in your everyday life.

Some of the readings are long, while others are short.
Some are my own original words, while others are penned by my friends.
Some guide you towards answers, while others may leave you with more questions.
Some include passages of scripture, while others do not.
I challenge you to find the truth of scripture in each of them even if it is not clearly laid out. As Augustine said,
All truth is God's truth.

For me, the truths I hold deepest and dearest are the ones I uncovered, dug up, and tasted myself rather than the ones handed to me on a perfectly prepared platter.

I challenge you to use these words as a diving board from which to jump into a deeper place in God's word. Let him lead you there. He knows what you need and how you need to receive it. Trust him.

Ultimately, I find my purpose aligns with that of one of my favorite theologians, Dallas Willard.

...a widespread transformation of character through wisely disciplined discipleship to Christ can transform our world...can disarm the structural evils that have always dominated humankind and now threaten to destroy the earth.

So while I write to teach, to add to our knowledge,
my ultimate aim is to change our practice radically.

4

A change of mind or heart means nothing if it doesn't change your life. I can't change your life, but I can point you to the One who can. His is the voice I want you to hear above all the rest.

Our world is loud. We aren't always sure which voices to listen to. Which ones will guide us along a path of purpose? Which ones are leading straight towards a dead end?

Only the voice of God can be trusted all the time, every time. To hear his voice, we must be familiar with how he speaks. To be familiar with how he speaks, we must listen to the ways he has spoken. To listen to the ways he has spoken, we must dig into his story – the one he has been writing since the beginning of time until today. Spiritual disciplines will allow us to live within God's story and thereby train our ears to recognize the sound of his voice.

If you can hear him, you can follow him.
And that's when things really get good.

Thanks for beginning with me, friend.
xoxo, Elizabeth

~~~

begin.

It seems like the simplest place for us to start,
but there is one simpler.

be.

If getting into God's presence seems overwhelming,
remember this: all you have to do is *be.*

being is ***begin*** rearranged.

Let's get rearranged.
Let's set the lists and longings aside
and focus on ***being*** before we ***begin.***

We don't need to achieve the gift of God's presence.
That offering has already been made.
We simply need to become aware of it.

~~~

God beneath you,
God in front of you,
God behind you,
God above you,
God within you.
{Saint Patrick}

PART I

Rhythms and Racehorses

~Understanding Spiritual Disciplines~

To fall in love with God is the greatest romance; to seek him the greatest adventure; to find him, the greatest human achievement.
— **Augustine**

CHAPTER 1
Composing Your Song

I sit cross-legged in an oversized chair at our family farmhouse. I am tucked away in the upstairs bedroom pecking away at my keyboard, writing this love offering you now hold in your hands. The walls are covered in white shiplap and the bed is an antique four poster. Outside, horses dot the pasture and flowers lay a colorful carpet along the edge of the house. There is no better place for inspiration and peaceful contemplation than the farm. Well, sort of. In a perfect world, I guess.

The truth is – it's not all peace and quiet here. At the moment there is an epic sibling squabble taking place downstairs. I have had to endure the frantic knocking on the door every 5 minutes and the echoes of arguments trailing up the stairwell. I heard something spill, but I've decided it doesn't matter if I clean it up now or later. You've been in this place haven't you? Maybe not the same surroundings, but similar conditions.

Sometimes we have something we so desperately want to accomplish and we just can't find a nice quiet place to accomplish it. That's my life. But I'm learning to be patient and keep trudging along. Even if I'm positive I will be interrupted and I'm not sure when it will be complete, I'm learning to begin anyway. It is the simplest and hardest part of many things we set out to do. We can't always wait for the perfect conditions so we start where we are, use what we have, and do what we can. You might be surprised where that leads you.

Maybe you are a student with a ton of homework, or a young professional clocking overtime, or a mama of a tiny one who keeps you up all hours of the night, or a referee of sibling squabbles, or a caregiver for your aging parents. Whatever life has piled on your plate; we can't wait for the perfect conditions.

A full life is good, but be careful what you fill it with. Yes, there are things out of our control we must tend to, but if we're honest there are minutes and hours in our days we have a say in. Anything of value requires us to spend it wisely. We can't make time, but we can't make excuses either. If something is important, it deserves a slot on our calendars.

There will be time, depend on it, for everything *God wants us to do.*
~ Elisabeth Elliot, "Discipline: The Glad Surrender"

If you're looking for direction in your life,
if you need advice for making a big decision,
if you want someone to tell you what in the world your current crisis is all about,
I am not your girl.

But I know someone. And he has been so reliable, wise, and kind in providing the direction and purpose for my own life that I want to take you to Him.

As you step further and further into the pages of this book you may learn something, but more importantly I hope you will go somewhere. The words I have written are meant to lead you, not to a specific place, but to an increased awareness of God's presence.   As D.T. Niles said,
I am a beggar, telling the other beggars
where to find bread.

I can't give you what you need to live the life God is calling you to –
only He can do that. I can simply point you in the right direction. I have invited a few of my friends along so that, together, we might tell you what a life spent in the presence of God has looked like for us.

I am desperate for you to acknowledge Him and spend purposeful time with Him. Once you are there – really there – He will do the work He intends to do in your heart and your life. And when He does, my prayer is that you will be compelled to get other people into that place too. Let's all keep grabbing hands and leading the way back home.

It seems so simple, doesn't it?

Just get in his presence.
Just carve out the time.
Just make it a priority.

But, y'all, we are going to have to fight for it! I'm telling you right now. This world has so much evidence of the divine, but there are so many distractions keeping us away. The distractions will be our default if we do not commit to seeing past them, to shutting them out, to wading through the mud and muck to get to deeper waters of clarity and truth. In his book "Secrets of the Secret Place", Bob Sorge says,

> ...the power of heaven is unlocked on earth when we devote
> ourselves to the secret place of the Most High...Hell will do
> everything in its power to misrepresent and distort the exuberant
> delight of this dynamic reality; this present world system is
> strategically designed to squeeze out your time and energy for the
> secret place; the church usually focuses its best energies on getting
> saints busy; and there seem to be relatively few believers whose
> secret life with God is so vibrantly life-giving that it kindles a
> contagious desire in others to follow their example.

Devotion. It is up to us to be devoted to attuning ourselves to the sacred over and over again. God's presence is our protection from a world that will draw us into a tumultuous tide of half-truths and hurts, knocking us down and taking us under, as we gasp for air. Or, worse, we will sit rocking in the boat until waves of complacency lull us to sleep and we are tossed overboard to drown in a sea of passivity.

~~~

My son, Oliver, has musical gifts straight from God. They certainly didn't come from me or his tone-deaf daddy. When Oliver figured out how to play the Star Wars theme song by ear at age six on a 6-inch plastic keyboard, we were amazed. We found this angel of a piano teacher – Ms. Rachel – and have watched our boy spread his musical wings ever since. Even though I can't really carry a tune, I've learned a lot about music sitting on Ms. Rachel's couch during lessons.

Music is built on the interplay of melody, harmony and rhythm. Melody is what results from playing notes in an organized way. Melodies are very distinguishable. They are the part of the song you typically sing. They tend to stand out and say something over the course of the song – either with words or notes. Melodies communicate.

Harmony is a complement to the melody. It hangs back. It's not the star of the show, but is of equal importance. Multiple notes played together as chords make up the harmony. They serve as a foundation, a support. Harmony helps the melody shine.

Rhythm is the movement of the music. The tempo, or speed, and beat, contribute to the rhythm. The melody and harmony ride on the rhythm.

Some people talk about spiritual disciplines as a rhythm. I see the connection. It's not an incorrect comparison. But here's the thing. A constant rhythm can put me to right to sleep. I'm just being honest. A beating heart. A driving rain. They are comforting sounds that bring peace and rest. I like comfort and peace. I also like sleeping, but I don't want to sleep through my life.

If we're not careful, spiritual disciplines can become too much of a steady rhythm that eventually goes unnoticed. There is no energy connecting us to them anymore. There is no melody telling a story or harmony making that story shine.

For me, spiritual disciplines must be more than a rhythm.

~~~

After a year of lessons, Oliver began to complain about practicing. What had once been fun and exciting had become boring drudgery for him. I knew music could ultimately be something very important in his life, so I hated to see him give up so easily. I shared my concern with Ms. Rachel. She knew exactly what to do.

The following week when we arrived for Oliver's lesson, the front door was cracked open. As we made our way up the steps and onto the porch a glorious sound filled our ears. Oliver and I looked at each other and smiled. We stood at the door for a moment and watched as Ms. Rachel's fingers danced across the keys producing perfection. When she heard us she paused and turned to Oliver with a grin. She invited him over to the bench beside her and asked if he heard what she was playing. He nodded his head. She went on to explain that it was part of a song she had composed herself. Oliver sat wide-eyed listening as Ms. Rachel told him she believed he was ready to begin composing his own song too.

I will always look back on that day as a turning point. It was the day music became more than something to sit down and learn. It became something he could dive into and create.

Over the past year I have watched Oliver compose his first song. He has considered melody, harmony and rhythm along with a dozen other nuances of music. I never realized the complexity of a single song before witnessing this process. I have seen his complaining and complacency replaced with engagement and excitement.

You cannot be a passive participant when it comes to composing music. The same goes for composing a life in Christ. You must write a melody to communicate. You must build a harmony to support it. You must calculate the rhythm to carry it. And, most important of all, you must regularly position yourself in front of the keys and listen.

You may think musicians must play a tune before they hear it, but, at least in Oliver's case, I have found the opposite to be true. He hears first, plays later.

I noticed this the first day he sat down to craft a simple melody. The melody was where Ms. Rachel had instructed him to begin. Once he was on the bench, in front of the keys, he momentarily closed his eyes as if searching for something. He seemed to be eliminating distractions *around* him so that he might find what he was looking for *within* him.

It was a picture of what spiritual disciplines have been for me.

We must first get in the listening place. We begin to hear that story-song from its source. At first we are the only ones who can hear it. Then we find a way to share it with others. For Oliver it traveled through his fingers, to the keys, and across the soundwaves to my ears.

Did you hear that Mommy?
Doesn't that sound good?

It did.

God has a life he wants to compose just for you. Do you hear it? Position yourself. Close your eyes. Listen. And then share your song with the world.

What has rocked you to sleep? Are you ready to wake up yet?

What has stolen your attention and affection? Are you ready to turn away?

If you know things need to change and you're desperate for a new rhythm of life that offers room to breathe instead of a stale suffocating space, you've come to the right place. I travel all over the country sharing the beauty and truth of the gospel with others. At every stop along the way I get the same question. When we have spent a weekend, or a day, or even just an hour diving deeper into God's word, their beaming faces look to me and ask – *what's next?* Every time we walk from the shallow waters of spirituality to the depths of abundant living, there is a yearning for more.

Of course there is.

That yearning is not the result of my perfect preparation, but of God's perfect presence. And so I want us there – every. single. day.

> *Your word is a lamp to my feet and a light to my path.*
> {Psalm 119:105, ESV}

Let's travel that path together. Don't stop just because your Bible study came to an end or the weekend retreat is over or the church service concluded. No speaker or writer or pastor or counselor can give you what you most need. Stop looking to us for the things we do not possess. The best I can do is this...

I can take your hand and gently guide you. I can dip my own cupped hand into the living water. I can hold that water up to your lips and watch the quenching of your thirst. I can do that. It is my honor to do that. But what you receive, what keeps you coming back for more is what God provides you in those moments. What he provides is - Himself.

When you ask *what's next* I know you want more of those moments, more of Him. You want a consistent diet of truth and beauty prepared by God himself and served up to you every day. I don't want you to lose that hunger. I don't want you to find a substitute thirst quencher. So I wrote this book.

I could never preach enough sermons or write enough Bible studies to give others everything their souls need. God may speak through me momentarily, but we were meant for more than a moment. We were meant for an eternal relationship.

Relationship is day after day, week after week, year after year of showing up.
Relationship is making time and space for what matters most.
Relationship is listening and learning and sharing and growing.
Relationship is messy and unpredictable.
And God wants every bit of that with us.

Now before you go getting all overwhelmed on me, listen. The relationship will come if we are willing to simply *begin.*

This book is a beginning, but not just a one-time beginning.
As St. Benedict said,
Always we begin again.

This is the heart of the gospel of Jesus Christ. Grace means we get another chance, and another and another and another. It doesn't mean we do whatever we want. It means when we seek to follow God's plans for our lives we won't get it right every time and we will need to come back around and try again. We will need to push the reset button.

When I drag myself out of the bed every morning to get in God's presence before I allow myself into anyone else's presence, I am pushing the reset button. I am willing myself out from under the warm cozy covers at an ungodly hour, pulling on a sweater, shuffling down the hall, and putting myself in position to begin again.

Beginnings are important. They determine how we will end.

So whether we are beginning our day or beginning a project or beginning a new stage of life, the way we begin matters. Will our pride set us on the fast track, believing we can figure everything out on our own? Or, in humility, will we take the time to have grace and truth poured into us before we dare to pour anything out?

I have a terrible tendency to get too far ahead of myself. I am always at risk of traveling to Egypt when God has plans for me in Kansas. However, a wise person once said: *Begin with the end in mind.* Now, hold on just a minute. I didn't say: *Begin with the end on your to-do list for the day.* Having the end in mind is very different from having the end in hand before the sun goes down. We can carry our purpose and our ultimate destination in our minds, but there are many steps between here and there to be guided and taken with great care.

~~~

begin.

No carefully thought out 5-year plan. No Bible reading schedule or small group curriculum.

Just - begin...period.

One of the greatest hindrances to our spiritual growth is our failure to launch. Fear and doubt tell us we have no idea where to actually begin, and so we don't do anything at all. We get stuck somewhere in between a momentary experience with the living God and the hope of an abundant, eternal life with him.

Maybe you're new to this whole spiritually healthy, soul-keeping, Bible studying thing. Maybe you got a good taste but now it seems the kitchen closed. Maybe you feasted on the truth of Scripture for years and walked hand-in-hand with Jesus but somewhere along the way something happened and you can't find your way back. Maybe you're just hungry and worn out. Maybe you have no idea 'what' you are, but you sure would like to move forward.

What if we all just stood up, looked each other in the eyes and agreed to take a step. Not a step towards another cause or another fight, but a step towards truth. A truth to guide us in our fighting and our surrendering, in our 'taking a stand' and our 'taking a seat'. The precious, grace-filled truth of God's word is the most solid thing I can offer you in this shaky, uncertain world.

The bad news is: I have no idea where the pages of this book will take each one of you. The good news is: God does.
The bad news is: I can't write a perfect storybook ending for your life. The good news is: I can help you turn the page to the next chapter.

begin.

No big, fancy capital letter. Just a simple step. Over and over and over again.

It's amazing really. When we just 'begin' in our spiritual journey we will also find ourselves just beginning in our real world living too.

That group you wanted to start?
That project you've considered attempting?
That conversation you've been dying to have?
That book you wanted to write?
That relationship you need to pursue?

When you get in the habit of beginning with Christ, it won't just happen behind closed doors between the two of you, it will spill over into your everyday, ordinary life.

Remember, this is a relationship. A relationship isn't confined to a certain place or time or season. A relationship is lived out, influencing all aspects of your life. If you begin to cultivate your

18

relationship with Jesus, you will cultivate a 'begin' mentality for all aspects of your life. You will find you have the courage and wisdom to take beginning steps in all kinds of places, because you are not alone. You are no longer flying solo because you have allowed someone else into the pilot's seat. I know my place when I know his.

Follow first, lead later. That's a good place to start.

We must know before we can love.
In order to know God, we must often think of Him;
and when we come to love Him,
we shall then also think of Him often,
for our heart will be with our treasure.
~ Brother Lawrence, "The Practice of the Presence of God"

CHAPTER 2
The Starting Line

I sat in the driver's seat of my minivan with my hand pressed up to the glass. I felt the chill hugging the other side of the window. It was barely above freezing on that late January morning, but inside I was comfortable, cozy even. I was parked in a sunny spot on the street in front of my parents' house. The windows held the cold at a distance as the warmth gently made its way through. From that spot I could see a camellia bush bravely displaying her pink blooms, despite the harsh conditions surrounding her. I felt inspired. I felt ready. But I knew I wasn't. Not just yet.

The day had been circled on my calendar for weeks – 'writing day'. I don't get many of those so I was eager to get to work. There was a quiet room waiting on me inside the house, but I held myself back like a horse in the gate. I was so ready to race off and into the work. It was a good work - a kingdom work. But it was still work, which meant I must exercise caution. I waited for the stillness to settle over me. Like a trainer's hand softly, but thoroughly, running itself along my side, God brought my focus back to him and off of the race ahead. On the other side of the gate I would break free and tear towards the finish line, but first I had to stop, look, and listen to the one who holds the secret to winning. I swear I need blinders.

It's the story of my life really. With all the lists and longings I wake up holding in my hands each day, there seems to be no time for the resting. My feet hit the ground running. I am worse than a workhorse. I am a racehorse. Every day there is a new finish line to cross. Every night I lay down in exhaustion. Little by little the disintegration of my soul takes place. The part of me that
wants to play,
needs to gaze,
longs to slow,
tries to grow,
smells the flowers,

sits for hours...

The part of me that survives by *being* instead of *doing* gets neglected – forgotten altogether.

Spiritual amnesia. I forget. I am forgotten. Not by God, but by myself. Somewhere along the way I lose my true self. And when I lose my true self I have lost my connection to the One who created my true self. Only time in the truth can bring me back – to myself and to my God.

With fatherly wisdom he reminds me,

> *Your salvation requires you to turn back to me*
> *and stop your silly efforts to save yourselves.*
> *Your strength will come from settling down*
> *in complete dependence on me –*
> *the very thing you've been unwilling to do.*
> *You've said, 'We'll rush off on horseback!'*
> *You'll rush off, all right! Just not far enough!*
> *You've said, 'We'll ride off on fast horses!'*
> *Do you think your pursuers ride old nags? Think again:*
> *A thousand of you will scatter before one attacker.*
> *Before a mere five you'll all run off.*
> *There'll be nothing left of you – a flagpole on a hill with no flag,*
> *a signpost on a roadside with the sign torn off.*
> {Isaiah 30:15-17}

Time taunts and teases us. It offers half-truths as it chases us down biting our heels. But God...

> *But God's not finished. He's waiting around to be gracious to you.*
> *He's gathering strength to show mercy to you. God takes the time*
> *to do everything right – everything.*
> {verse 18}

We spend time like money and it always feels like our bank account is depleted. When we can't tame it, we waste it – give up on trying. But God *takes* time. He takes it right into his hands. He bends it and shapes it and uses it perfectly. He creates a rhythm with the hours, days, weeks, years and invites us to fall into it. We can't catch time and we can't outrun it. The control of it will always elude us. And so we release our grip on that ticking hand, and let God lead us into what is right instead of time dragging us down into everything that's wrong.

We weren't meant to race from sun-up to sun-down. We run ourselves ragged, and for what? In the end there is nothing useful left of us. What is a flagpole without a flag? What is a signpost without a sign? The message we are meant to offer the world, the truth we are meant to share with our neighbors, the beauty we are meant to paint with our lives is lost when we run without rest. We fail to serve our sacred purpose in this world when we are too quick out of the gate. We find ourselves injured, disqualified, breathless and burned out.

For nearly a decade now I have been learning how to discipline myself at the starting line of each day. I have pleaded with others to join me on the journey because there has been nothing of greater importance in my life than how I begin. Anything of lasting value in our lives is only cultivated as a response to having heard from God first. If we don't know how to listen for his voice, we will find ourselves taking instruction from other far less qualified sources.

Whether you are like me – a horse anxious to break free from the gate – or like some of my friends – spooked and afraid to take the next galloping step towards their dreams – the starting line is the same. How we begin is important. It will determine how we end. And so together we will find purpose and a plan for how we begin each day, each project, each dream we've been carrying inside of us.

~~~

The most frequently quoted passage from the Old Testament of the Bible is this,

> *For I know the plans I have for you, declares the Lord, plans to prosper you and not to harm you, plans to give you hope and a future.*
> {Jeremiah 29:11, NIV}

It is a lovely and encouraging sentiment, but it is misunderstood if taken out of context. God was talking to a group of people who had been exiled. They were far from home. Life had not gone according to plan. They were most likely very disappointed and discouraged.

The prosperity.
The hope.
The future.

Those were all things to come. In the moment there was only suffering, confusion, and compromise. But, when the time was right, God would work it all for good on one condition. Yes, there is a condition. No, God's love for us is not conditional, but his ability to bring about his very best in our lives is conditional. God's best for us is conditional upon our cooperation.

> *Then you will call upon me and come and pray to me, and I will hear you.*
> {verse 12}

Call upon him. Come to him. Pray to him.

> *You will seek me and find me, when you seek me with all your heart. I will be found by you, declares the Lord, and I will restore your fortunes and gather you from all the nations and all the places where I have driven you, declares the Lord, and I will bring you back to the place from which I sent you into exile.*
> {verses 13-14}

24

This is how the Message translation puts it.

When you come looking for me, you'll find me. Yes, when you get serious about finding me and want it more than anything else, I'll make sure you won't be disappointed.

{Jeremiah 29:13}

Disappointment. *A feeling of sadness or displeasure caused by the nonfulfillment of one's hopes or expectations.*

If hope is a balloon, disappointment is the pin to pierce it. Deflated. Fallen.

You've been there, haven't you? Whether it was an event, a person, or even a season of life – disappointment has found you.

We are hard-wired to seek, to search. We are looking for something, someone, that will not disappoint. Everything we uncover falls short. Temporary satisfaction gives way to unmet long-term expectations. The happiness wanes. The pleasure subsides. The good feeling turns bad. The search continues. We are sure it is hiding out there somewhere – the one thing that will not disappoint.

But what if the hope that will not disappoint looks different than we expected? What if it is beyond anything we could ever imagine yet very much within our reach? What if it's not something 'out there' but something closer than the air we breathe? What if we've made the search so complicated but it is really quite simple? As simple as opening a door.

~~~

When I was a child my family would attend my mother's family reunion every summer. It was a weekend full of fun. Our whole great big family stayed at the only hotel in the small town of Manning, South Carolina. It was one of those one story buildings in the shape of a square with a pool in the middle. I think it's been condemned now, but at the time I thought it was spectacular. It was the first time

I remember seeing adjoining rooms. You've probably stayed in one before. There are two doors, back to back, in the wall between the rooms. At our reunion we would sometimes get lucky and stay next door to our cousins. Very exciting. If it were up to the kids the doors would stay open the entire time. Unfortunately, it wasn't always up to the kids. There were many times when I would excitedly open the door on our side of the wall only to find the door from the other side locked up tight. Even though it was just a matter of privacy I couldn't help but feeling rejected, left out. Talk about disappointment.

You may have had the proverbial door slammed in your face a time or two. It hurts. The good news is – God's door is always open. If I ever sense a separation between me and God, it's because my side is closed.

By entering through faith into what God has always wanted to do for us—set us right with him, make us fit for him—we have it all together with God because of our Master Jesus. And that's not all: We throw open our doors to God and discover at the same moment that he has already thrown open his door to us.
We find ourselves standing where we always hoped we might stand—out in the wide open spaces of God's grace and glory, standing tall and shouting our praise.
There's more to come: We continue to shout our praise even when we're hemmed in with troubles, because we know how troubles can develop passionate patience in us, and how that patience in turn forges the tempered steel of virtue, keeping us alert for whatever God will do next. In alert expectancy such as this, we're never left feeling shortchanged. Quite the contrary— we can't round up enough containers to hold everything God generously pours into our lives through the Holy Spirit!
{Romans 5:1-5}

~ ~ ~

When my children were tiny they discovered the game of 'Hide and Seek'. Honestly, they weren't very good at it. I humored them by pretending I couldn't see their heads peeking out from underneath the bed or their little fingers curled around the edge of the curtain. God plays hide and seek like a toddler. He wants to be found. He's not trying to trick you. He's got his eye on you in all of your wandering. He's grinning and giddy with excitement at the prospect of your gaze meeting his.

On the other side of that door you've closed – his is wide open.

This book is about opening the door. This book is about settling in at the starting gate before we go racing off toward the finish line. This book is about seeking and finding. Not once. Not just at the beginning of your faith, but over and over again for the rest of your life. It's something worth getting serious about. It's the only thing that won't disappoint us.

Maybe you're like me. Maybe you find yourself asking God over and over again to show you the next step. Maybe instead of asking for the next step we simply need to take the first one.

If we seek, we will find. And when the time is right, all of God's promises will be fulfilled. What's to come is more abundant and extravagant than you could ever imagine. But we will miss it if we don't know the One who can lead us there. When you go looking for him you will find - he's been looking for you all along. The exiles and I can both testify to this truth.

They found grace out in the desert, these people who survived the killing. Israel, out looking for a place to rest, met God out looking for them! God told them, 'I've never quit loving you and never will. Expect love, love, and more love! And so now I'll start over with you and build you up again.

*You'll resume your singing, grabbing tambourines and joining the
dance. You'll go back to your old work of planting vineyards on the
Samaritan hillsides, and sit back and enjoy the fruit –
oh, how you'll enjoy those harvests!'*
{Jeremiah 31:2-5}

Oh friends, I know you've known disappointment. I know you've
experienced the killing – of jobs and homes and relationships and
children and parents and dreams. But you've survived and you're
looking for rest and rejoicing. There's only one place to find it.
There's only one place to be lavished in love and sent back on your
way to reap the harvests of God-ordained work.

Grab your tambourines.
Raise your voices.
Join the dance.

The eternal love of God is waiting to build you up and send you out
again and again and again.

CHAPTER 3
His Commandment, Our Commitment

Jesus didn't stand behind a podium or a microphone when he addressed groups of people. Often a boat served as his stage while his audience listened from the shorelines. Conditions need not be perfect to share what God has put on your heart. Jesus demonstrated that wherever you are, whatever you've got, you can just begin. And Jesus often began with a story.

One day the story began like this. *

A farmer planted seeds...

Jesus went on to describe where the seeds fell. Some fell on the road where the birds promptly ate them. Some fell in gravel where they actually sprouted up but didn't put down roots, so the sun caused them to wither right away. Some fell in weeds where they were strangled as soon as they began to grow. And some fell on good, fertile soil. These seeds were the only ones to produce a harvest. In fact, Matthew tells us the harvest was beyond the farmer's wildest dreams.

I'm going to ask you the same question Jesus asked at the end of this story.

Are you listening to this? Really listening?

If I want to know if my children have really listened to a story I have told, I ask them specific questions about it. Here's what I would ask you about this story.

Where would you want your seeds to fall?
Would you like for something to happen that is beyond your wildest dreams?

*Matthew Ch. 13

29

If the answer to the second question is 'yes' then you know the answer to the first question as well. Your seeds need to fall on fertile ground. OK. But how? How do we make sure all the seeds we sow in our lives are not going to be eaten by enemies, or withered by harsh conditions, or strangled by worry?

Jesus lays out the answer for his disciples and for us.

Sowing your seeds in good soil means taking in the truth of God's word so it might fertilize the soil of your soul, preparing it to produce a harvest. Jesus cautions against hearing God's word on a surface level but not actually taking it into a deeper place, leaving it susceptible to the Enemy. He warns of instantly and emotionally responding to God's word but not having any character to underlie the emotion. When the emotion is gone and conditions grow hard, nothing remains. He also alerts them to the possibility of their own worries and cares strangling anything good that might initially come from the seed.

I have sown my seeds on the road, in the gravel, and amongst weeds. I have a feeling you have too. I also have a feeling, like me, you desire to see growth and the production of fruit in your life. Wasted seeds are not just seeds. They are time and energy and resources we have been given. We don't want to squander them. Here's the good news. Stick your hand down in your pocket. Do you feel that? There are still seeds to be sown.

When you look at your own life, where do you find most of your seeds falling? And how do we get more of them into fertile soil? How do we get ourselves there?

Jesus talks to the disciples about having eyes to see and ears to hear. This is what I desperately want for you and for me. I want us to find the truth within the story. Throughout the scriptures it is clear that those who have eyes to see and ears to hear have one thing in common. They are close to Jesus. The closer they are to Jesus, the clearer they see. The deeper their relationship with the Savior, the louder his voice can be heard in their ears.

Later, Jesus lays out for his disciples and for us what bearing fruit really looks like. He says it simply.

Love God and love others. *

In my experience and the experience of nearly every fruit-bearing person I have met in the scriptures and in real life, bearing fruit **begins** with loving God and **leads** to loving others. This book would be incomplete if I did not make that point. Spiritual disciplines put us in position to develop a loving relationship with God, but we cannot stop there. The result of that loving relationship with God is a loving relationship with others.

That, Jesus says, is the greatest commandment.

And it will require your greatest commitment.

Greater than your commitment to your job
Redecorating your home
Making money
Taking care of your children
Achieving fame and fortune

If your goal is the greatest of all commandments, it will require the greatest of all commitments.

And that means getting the condition of the soil of souls right.

This is what it means to be a disciple of Jesus.

It's not showing up at church on Sundays. It's not memorizing the Lord's prayer. It's not checking off your community service

* Mark 12:30-31

requirements. It's not saying a blessing before meals. It is your life.

~~~

When I was a children's ministry pastor I wrote a book for the families in our church. On the first page of that book was a letter to parents. One of the lines was intended to say,
We are excited to partner with you in discipling your children,
but well-intentioned spellcheck got me in trouble once again by changing the sentence to say,
We are excited to partner with you in <u>disciplining</u> your children.

I'm not sure parents appreciated the image of me standing over their children with a wooden spoon. But you can see how easily the mistake was made and how I missed it in the final edits before the book was printed.

Discipline and *Disciple* are awfully close, and with good reason.
As a disciple of Jesus we should reflect the discipline of Jesus.

Traditionally, disciplines fall into two categories – disciplines of abstinence and disciplines of engagement. We will begin with the one most people find most difficult. It may surprise you to know that disciplines requiring little or nothing of us are actually harder for us to implement than the ones requiring greater time and energy.

Remember that horse raring to go behind the gate? Maybe that's you right now. I know, I know. It's me too. But we're going to stay in that restricted space for a bit longer while we learn to stop before we get started.

There are seeds in our pockets and we need some direction on where and when to toss them.

CHAPTER 4
The Enemy of All Disciplines

When John Ortberg asked the great theologian Dallas Willard for his greatest bit of wisdom related to soul care he said this, and only this,

You must ruthlessly eliminate hurry from your life. *

{Insert sucker punch}

The first time I read those words they literally took my breath away. God had pressed his finger into a bleeding wound in my soul. I knew what was preventing me from moving forward in all other aspects of my spiritual growth. My attempts at spiritual disciplines would fail if I did not commit to this one thing.

Hurry.

Eliminate it.

That day my husband and I committed to wrestle hurry to the ground in the life of our family. We would no longer live without margin, allowing hurry to bully us into disobedient and disgruntled behaviors. As an achievement-driven racehorse, this was no easy feat for me. My identity was tied up in my productivity and that had to change.

In order to eliminate hurry, you must be able to identify it. It helps to understand the difference between being hurried and being busy.

Hurry is driven by pride. Busy is driven by passion with purpose.
Hurry gets offended. Busy has time for you and doesn't see you as an inconvenience or obstacle to get past.
Hurry is focused so much on the future that it misses the present and those within it. Busy knows where we are headed is important, but not at the expense of where we are right now.

* Ortberg, John. *Soul Keeping.* Zondervan, 2014.

Jesus was busy, but he never seemed to be in a hurry. Jesus always had time for others. He also had time for God. We will take a closer look at this in the next chapter, but before we take another step let's commit to this one thing. <u>Identify hurry in your life and eliminate it.</u> Put it in a choke hold and wrestle it to the ground until it doesn't have an ounce of power over you anymore.

I will warn you. Hurry will eventually catch its breath and get back up and after you. But you will begin to recognize the sound of its footsteps creeping up behind you. You will hear them echoing in your chest as your heart rate increases and your blood pressure rises. You will recognize the shift in your tone of voice and the tensing of muscles that follows. You will recognize the patterns and places in which it makes its most frequent appearances. Hurry holds hands with anger and resentment, so be on guard when they make an appearance.

Hurry meets me most often right by my back door next to the pile of shoes missing their mates and the coat rack void of coats, where the children suddenly begin moving like sloths and the words come bubbling up like a poison in my chest – HURRY UP!!!

It happens y'all. Hurry finds us. But we don't have to carry him around on our back all day. Take a deep breath, shed him from your shoulders and remember – there is no place you are going or thing you are doing that is more important than the people you may roll right over to get there. And that includes yourself.

No. more. hurry.

The first step to eliminating hurry is examining our calendars. Just as books need margins in which we can jot notes and pause to contemplate something unexpected, our life needs margin too. If the words were crammed on the page – top to bottom and left to right – we would feel overwhelmed. There would be no space to consider our own thoughts, our own response to what we encounter along the way. {Side note: Please write in this book. Please underline and highlight and jot down notes. They might come in handy later.}

When my calendar is crammed I feel the same pressing. There is no room to pause and respond to what we encounter along the way. There is no time to have an important, impromptu conversation with someone who crosses our path. There is no space to sit in our cars for a few moments to allow our blood pressure to slow before we step into that next appointment. There is no opportunity for stillness and space, only movement without margin.

Before beginning the practice of spiritual disciplines, you will most likely have to quit something {or some things}. You are definitely going to have to learn how to say 'no', and remember that the world will *not* stop turning if you don't sign up for every meal train and every committee that comes your way.

Yes, I know that may sound selfish. I guilted myself into doing everything for everybody for years. Then God showed me the sin of pride hidden beneath my constant willingness to help and serve. Not all *good* things are *God* things. I've learned to change the question I ask when deciding what to say 'yes' and 'no' to.

Instead of asking myself – Is this something I *could* do?
I ask God – Is this something I *should* do?

When I say 'yes' to something God intended for me to say 'no' to, I am not only being disobedient, I am setting myself up for a margin-less life of hurry that keeps me focused on all the wrong things. God's best for me and those around me will never be found in that place. The enemy loves to keep us busy doing all the wrong things for all the wrong reasons.

I remind myself over and over again to heed this warning by Ruth Haley Barton in her book "Sacred Rhythms",

Many of us try to shove spiritual transformation into the nooks and crannies of a life that is already unmanageable, rather than being willing to arrange our life for what our heart most wants. We think that somehow we will fall into transformation by accident.

No more shoving and stuffing. God doesn't fit in a box. Now that we are ready to make room and take time let's discover together what intentional practice of spiritual disciplines might look like in our lives.

WARNING:
As you read through each of the disciplines outlined in this book, PLEASE resist the temptation to begin practicing them all at once. The next two chapters should be read for a beginner's understanding and increased awareness of how God may guide you in your spiritual journey. Once you get into the daily readings you can begin practicing some of the disciplines. You may choose to focus on one for a while and then move on. You may integrate a few together and then re-evaluate. The point is to begin composing your life song. This will not happen overnight.
Be patient and alert. God will guide you.

CHAPTER 5
Disciplines of Abstinence

If we feel that any habit of pursuit, harmless in itself, is keeping us from God and sinking us deeper in the things of earth; if we find that things which others can do with impunity are for us the occasion of falling, then abstinence is our only course. Abstinence alone can recover for us the real value of what should have been for our help but which had been an occasion of falling. It is necessary that we should steadily resolve to give up anything that comes between ourselves and God.
~ W. R. Inge

I may be slightly immature. Every time I hear the word 'abstinence' I giggle a little inside. It is my inner 4th grader sitting alongside my friends on the floor of a church classroom during a weekend retreat on sex education.

Okay. Deep breath. Focus. Get past the middle school mentality.

Sex education may have made abstinence famous but we're going way beyond that here. Abstinence is getting rid of or avoiding something. If we remove a lesser thing we make room for more important things. Disciplines of abstinence may feel like we're not *doing* anything. But sometimes not doing something is the best thing you can do. And sometimes the *not* doing is more difficult than we'd like to admit.

A close look at Jesus' "great acts" of humility, faith, and compassion recorded in the Gospel narratives finds them to be moments in a life more pervasively and deeply characterized by solitude, fasting, prayer, and service. Surely, then, the lives of his followers must be just as deeply characterized by those same practices.
~ Dallas Willard, "The Spirit of the Disciplines"

As we examine some of the disciplines that will increase our intimacy with God and our involvement with his plans, Jesus will be our example.

SOLITUDE

During Jesus' ministry here on earth he attracted a lot of crowds. He was often surrounded by seas of people. But Jesus knew the importance of the first of our disciplines of abstinence, and we see him practice it over and over again.

With the crowd dispersed, he climbed the mountain so he could be by himself and pray. He stayed there alone, late into the night.
{Matthew 14:23}

While it was still night, way before dawn,
he got up and went out to a secluded spot and prayed.
{Mark 1:35}

As often as possible Jesus withdrew to out-of-the-way places
for prayer.
{Luke 5:16}

Solitude is making the choice to be alone. Sounds easy enough, but solitude is not only abstaining from the presence of others, but also the influence of others. If we want to set our course to seek the approval of God over the approval of man, this is imperative. If we want to hear straight from God and not receive some watered down, filtered out version of the truth, there is no substitute for solitude.

Do you think I speak this strongly in order to manipulate crowds?
Or curry favor with God? Or get popular applause? If my goal was
popularity, I wouldn't bother being Christ's slave.
Know this – I am most emphatic here, friends –
this great message I have delivered to you is not mere human
optimism. I didn't receive it through the traditions, and I wasn't
taught it in some school.

I got it straight from God, received the message directly
from Jesus Christ.
{Galatians 1:10-12}

At the risk of ruffling some feathers I am going to offer you this observation. Social media is killing the discipline of solitude for us! We don't know how to be alone. We go to the bathroom with our phones. {I've done it, y'all!} We respond to every ring and every ding. We let the FOMO {fear of missing out} drive us to regular Instagram and Facebook checks. We feel the need to constantly come up with creative ways to communicate with others on Snapchat. We set our phone alongside our Bible during our quiet time, allowing a whole world's worth of people access to us in what should be our secret place.

What if we got away from everyone else – both physically and virtually – at some point every day? What might God do in those sacred spaces of solitude?

Solitude is the foundation from which we will build a life of spiritual disciplines. Without it, anything else we construct will be prone to falling down. If solitude is particularly difficult for you, ask yourself why. Are you afraid of what you might find *within* yourself when you don't have distractions *around* yourself?

I know, dear one, it can be scary. I've been there. Solitude is the first step we are taking into deeper relationship with God, but I think we should pause because this is feeling very big to some of you.

Getting alone with anyone leads to one thing – intimacy. For some of you, intimacy has not been a safe place. For some of you, being vulnerable and releasing the grip on that mask you've held up to your face or that protection you've held around your body, has led to hurt and betrayal. It's time to let God redeem intimacy for you. It's time for you to know beyond a shadow of a doubt that he can be trusted with every single part of you. It's time to accept that you are wholly and completely loved by him. I know, because he has met me in my own places of betrayal and shame and fear, and revealed the freedom of true intimacy with him.

Can I let you in on a secret? All the years I avoided solitude, my internal life was wreaking havoc on my external life, and there was nothing I could do about it. I felt so broken, but I wasn't brave enough to actually examine the broken places and allow God to heal them. There are things we may not want to uncover, but uncover we must. Underneath the injuries are infinite depths of hope and possibility unlike anything you have ever known. Yes – right there inside of YOU. I promise. Don't be afraid to go there. I would go with you, but, well...that would defeat the purpose wouldn't it? But God is there. You are never alone. Even when you are alone.

Practicing solitude is as simple as going somewhere by yourself. Inside or outside, it doesn't matter. Just set your phone down and go there. And stay, for as long as it takes. Keep a journal and pen handy to record any discoveries. Feel free to pause and try it now, or wait until Part II of our book. You will have several guided opportunities then.

SILENCE
Silence is the way to make solitude a reality.
~ Henri Nouwen

Let's just be honest - this one does not come easy for me. Sometimes I ask God to speak up because I just want to hear him, so I can obey him. He lovingly whispers beneath the blanket of my busy-ness and bossiness – *I don't need to turn up the volume on my voice. You need to turn down the volume on your life.*

In returning and rest you shall be saved;
In quietness and in trust shall be your strength.
{Isaiah 30:15, NIV}

Silence often comes with solitude but the reverse may not always be true. The practice of silence is two-fold. We must learn to abstain {1} from the noise coming at us and {2} the noise coming from us. Silence is a discipline to be practiced while alone and also in the company of others.

> *Silence is not the absence of sound,*
> *but the absence of self.*
> ~ Anthony deMello

Developing an inner control and composure leads us away from our desire for external control over people and situations. There are times when someone is sharing something important with us and, despite our strong desire to spout out advice, we need to bite our tongues and listen. I know, it's hard. My mouth has been filled with blood plenty of times. But the truth is, with an ultimate goal of loving others we must learn how to not just be generous with our time and resources but also with our attention. Sometimes the greatest act of love and service comes in the form of a listening ear.

Silence in those situations will not only benefit others. Maybe, just maybe, we don't have it all figured out ourselves. And maybe, just maybe, when we shut our big mouths {which God has given us one of} we can use our ears {which God has given us two of} to gain wisdom. It's hard y'all. I know.

What if for a designated time every day we gave up the urge to control everyone and everything around us with our words and just sat silent and listened?
What if we actively sought out silence, coupled with solitude, by waking in the middle of the night or traveling to a deserted place to find true quiet and rest?

To practice silence, you can do one of two things:
{1} Start with solitude and don't say or listen to anything.
{2} In the company of others, abstain from pouring out your

thoughts and opinions and, instead, just listen.

FASTING/FRUGALITY

In its purest form fasting is about food or drink, but for simplicity's sake I am combining it with the discipline of frugality. In both cases we abstain from physical things that have become too important to us. Those things may be food and drink, but they may also be new shoes and fancy cars. The goal is to reveal what controls us and what has become too important.

Jesus lived a life of simplicity, free of designer clothes and a perfectly decorated home. Those things in and of themselves are not necessarily bad, but if they are held in a position of great importance, they threaten to de-throne God as lord of our lives. In addition to the lifestyle example Jesus set, he also taught his disciples about fasting from food. We see him do it himself in the wilderness.

> *Next Jesus was taken into the wild by the Spirit for the Test.*
> *The Devil was ready to give it. Jesus prepared for the Test*
> *by fasting forty days and forty nights.*
> {Matthew 4:1}

I find it fascinating that Jesus' preparation for a mental, physical, and spiritual test was not to carb load or get a lot of sleep or study really hard or buy a new outfit. Instead he fasted. We will talk more about this in the 'readings' section of the book, but it's worth noticing now. Sometimes when the world tells us we need more 'stuff' to succeed, we actually need less.

Have you ever said something like this – *Well, you may do that, but I could NEVER!*

Think about that one thing you could never do without and consider if maybe you should. Consider if it has become so important to you that it is crowding out other things of greater importance. This is one of the places the enemy can be most effective at keeping us from an intimate relationship with Jesus and a life of abundance. He pacifies us with 'good' things so that we miss out on the 'better' things.

C.S. Lewis says it this way,
It would seem that Our Lord finds our desires not too strong, but too weak. We are half-hearted creatures, fooling about with drink and sex and ambition when infinite joy is offered us, like an ignorant child who wants to go on making mud pies in a slum because he cannot imagine what is meant by the offer of a holiday at the sea. We are far too easily pleased.

Fasting and frugality can be practiced a variety of ways but here are a few to consider. Again, if you are not feeling overwhelmed with the information thus far, and God is nudging you in this direction, go ahead and try them. Or you can read through the suggestions and tuck them away for Part II.

{1} When faced with an important decision or task that requires you to be very aware of God's presence and direction abstain from certain food and/or drink for a designated amount of time.

{2} Integrate fasting into your life on a more regular basis by picking one day per week or per month to abstain from certain food and/or drink and spend that time more focused on prayer and study.

One of my friends and mentors, Carol, chose Mondays as her fasting day when her children were young. She would abstain from any solid foods, partaking only of water and tea, throughout the day while her children were at school. During that time, she prayed and studied her Bible, cultivating an intimate relationship with Jesus. She broke fast at dinner time when she joined the rest of the family for a meal. The fruit of her life and her children's lives is evidence that this practice planted seeds deep in the soil of her faith and her family.

{3} Determine the one thing you believe you could never do without

{Netflix, dessert, coffee, shopping for clothes, etc.} and designate an amount of time to abstain from it. For example, several years ago a friend told me she had done a clothing fast. She did not purchase a single new item of clothing for 365 days. My first thought was – *that's ridiculous.* Then I realized my thought was actually ridiculous. Could I really not survive for a year on the closet full of clothes I already had at home? I took the challenge and I'm embarrassed to say, it was difficult *at first.* But, I could write an entire book about the unexpected benefits of that experience. It changed my life.

CHAPTER 6
Disciplines of Engagement

Now that we've hopefully found some stillness and surrender, it's time to engage. I've been chomping at the bit. Have you? Abstinence has made way for engagement. Disciplines of engagement will allow for some 'doing', but let's not take the reins back into our hands just yet. To be truly effective, the Holy Spirit will need to guide these practices as well. Don't go racing ahead too far.

STUDY

> *Every part of Scripture is God-breathed*
> *and useful in one way or another—*
> *showing us truth, exposing our rebellion, correcting our mistakes,*
> *training us to live God's way. Through the Word*
> *we are put together and shaped up for the tasks God has for us.*
> {2 Timothy 3:16}

If we are going to make our greatest commitment to the greatest commandment, we need to know what that looks like. How does God define that? How did Jesus live that out? These answers are found when we study the scriptures. Just as solitude is the foundation of disciplines of abstinence, study is the foundation of disciplines of engagement. If I could choose only one discipline for you to practice, it would be this one. It is a non-negotiable.

We live in an information age. Unlimited information is available to us all day, every day, in the form of books, magazines, blogs, apps, and websites. We can dig around all we want, looking for answers, but we are wasting our time if we have not dug our deepest holes in God's word. All other information is most useful when filtered through the truth of the Bible.

Jesus knew the importance of the scriptures. He was frequently heard quoting passages from the Old Testament. In fact, when asked about the greatest commandment, Jesus' response comes directly from the ancient text,

> *Love God, your God, with your whole heart:*
> *love him with all that's in you, love him with all you've got!*
> {Deuteronomy 6:5}

> *Don't seek revenge or carry a grudge against any of your people.*
> *Love your neighbor as yourself.* *I am God.*
> {Leviticus 19:18}

When Jesus faced trials and temptations directly from the devil in the desert he used scripture as his weapon. You will learn more about this in the 'readings' section of this book.

What if we committed to study and memorize one passage of scripture each month over the next year? As my wise, friend Deborah says, *When I really study a passage from God's word and apply it to my life – it becomes mine.* There is no greater tool than this.

I am not going to try and impress you with any big fancy words or techniques here. There is no right or wrong way to study your Bible. Just open it, or turn it on, and start reading. This is going to be a process. No two days ever look the same for me when it comes to Bible study.

In the begin.journal I outline something I call the 4 P's which I designed to help me study my Bible. You can also find a video describing the 4 P's on my website – www.elizabethmaxon.com Those may help, but in the meantime, here are some other tips for getting started. Feel free to try some now, or wait until we guide you through them in Part II.

{1} Read from the Message {MSG} translation.
{2} Read from The Jesus Storybook Bible by Sally Lloyd Jones. I promise that is not a joke or an insult. I read this Bible all the time. It tells the full story of God in a beautiful, engaging way.

{3} Read the verse of the day on the Bible App from YouVersion. Read it in at least 3 different translations.

{4} Read the book of John.

{5} Read a Psalm. If the first one you pick is weird, pick another one.

WORSHIP/CELEBRATION

In order to keep us moving along I have combined two important disciplines of engagement. Both worship and celebration are a response to what we learn, hear, taste, and see through the other disciplines.

Worship is the engagement and expression that often takes place as we get to know God personally through study. For me, worship is most often expressed through written words. Although I love singing praise songs in my car and at church {and occasionally the shower}, the one thing I am most compelled to do when I come face to face with the greatness of God is to write something to him or about him. On the regular, you can find me furiously scribbling down thoughts in the middle of a church service, or pulling up the voice recorder on my phone to capture a thought triggered when God reveals himself to me while driving down the road. I've also threatened to keep a dry erase marker in the shower because God tends to reveal some amazing things to me there.

Your expression of worship may look different. It may be painting or singing or speaking or running or a dozen other things. Any act compelled by a heart filled with wonder and awe at who God is, would be considered worship.

While worship typically occurs in the intimate space between you and God alone, celebration typically involves others. It is a favorite discipline for extroverts like me. Dallas Willard explains that celebration,

...is the completion of worship, for it dwells on the greatness of God as shown in his goodness to us.
We engage in celebration when we enjoy ourselves,

our life, our world, in conjunction with our
faith and confidence in God's greatness, beauty, and goodness.
We concentrate on our life and world
as God's work and his gift to us.

As you can see, both worship and celebration stem from a heart full of gratitude. When we focus on God's goodness we can focus on offering goodness back to him and others.

We've already established the importance of abstaining from things and practices that interfere with our relationship to God, but as with all disciplines, we should be careful not to swing the pendulum too far in one direction. If we find ourselves completely avoiding pleasure and delight, rather than just ensuring we are not dependent upon it, we are giving ourselves a spiritual death sentence.

Jesus, himself, described heaven as an elegant wedding banquet thrown by a king. In one of this parables, he explained that those who were too busy working to take time for celebrating outraged the king, and wound up missing the whole party. Don't be a party pooper.

In the words of Kool and the Gang – *celebrate good times, come on!*

This is your chance to get creative. Go ahead and be intentional about the disciplines of worship and celebration right now, or wait until we give you some specific prompts in Part II. Whenever and however you engage these disciplines – enjoy!

MEDITATION
I'd say you'll do best by filling your minds and meditating on things
true, noble, reputable, authentic, compelling, gracious –
the best, not the worst; the beautiful, not the ugly; things to praise,
not things to curse. Put into practice what you learned from me,
what you heard and saw and realized.

Do that, and God, who makes everything work together, will work
you into his most excellent harmonies.
{Philippians 4:8-9}

You can't think of nothing. I know that sounds grammatically
incorrect, like I'm some kind of country bumpkin. {I am from South
Carolina, y'all.} But, seriously, if you reread that statement, you'll
find it's true. At least it has been true for me. I have been unable to
clear my mind of everything. Meditation is not about emptying your
mind it is about filling it up with the right things.

There is an old proverb I love, which says,
Sow a thought, reap an act
Sow an act, reap a habit
Sow a habit, reap a character
Sow a character, reap a destiny.
Your destiny, your destination, begins with a thought. Wow.

Richard Foster explains meditation in his book "Celebration of the
Disciplines",
The purpose of meditation is to enable us to hear God more clearly.
Meditation is listening, sensing, heeding the life and light of Christ.
This comes right to the heart of our faith. The life that pleases God
is not a set of religious duties; it is to hear His voice and obey His
word. Meditation opens the door to this way of living.

In order to meditate on something, we are going to have to slow way
down and thoughtfully consider every word of what we read or hear.
We are going to dig for a deeper meaning. We are going to offer a
prayer to God that sounds something like this,
God – I know you have set your Spirit inside of me. I am asking
your Spirit to unlock for me the priceless treasure hidden within your
words.

Practicing solitude and silence alongside meditation is extremely
effective, but don't be limited to only the times and places you can be

alone. Sometimes you will need to utilize meditation in the middle of the loudest, craziest situations of your life. You will need to close your eyes and sink into a separate place, where the truth of God's word gives light in the middle of darkness. If you're a mom, the craziness may be your home and the loudness may be your children, and locking yourself in the bathroom may be the best you can do. You go right ahead and curl up in your bathtub and meditate, mama.

Set your mind on things that are above,
not on things that are on earth.
{Colossians 3:2}

We must take control of our thoughts. Whatever enters into our thinking must be evaluated and dealt with. Martin Luther once said, *You cannot keep birds from flying over your head, but you can keep them from building a nest in your hair.*

You will have the opportunity to practice meditation in Part II of the book, but here's a simple practice you can implement at any time. I call it the 'First-Last Thought'.

Choose a passage of scripture or a quote that expresses a truth of scripture. Spend some time reading the words carefully, praying over them, and letting God reveal the hidden secrets. Write the passage on an index card and sit it next to your bed. Let those words be your first thought when you wake up in the morning, and the last thought before you close your eyes at night. When your alarm goes off, don't reach for your phone. Reach for that card. When you get settled into bed, don't check Instagram one last time. Check your card. Let the truth seal your mind at the beginning and ending of every day. If you need some 'First-Last Thoughts' to get you started you can download some for free on my website.

PRAYER

The LORD is near to all who call upon Him,
to all who call upon Him in truth.
{Psalm 145}

I am not going to spend a lot of time on prayer. If it sounds too prescribed, I'm afraid you won't do it. God wants to hear <u>from</u> you and speak <u>to</u> you. That's the deal.

We all know about conversations. They are the exchange of words between two people. Have a conversation with God. Your words can be silent or spoken aloud. You can say them in the presence of others or when you are alone. If you've never tried it, I would recommend getting alone and speaking aloud. It can be powerful. Just don't forget to listen too.

Again, this is a discipline we see Jesus engage over and over again – when he's alone and when others are close to him.

Prayer invites God into the circumstances of our lives and gives us an awareness of His presence. Like the discipline of study, it is another non-negotiable of spiritual growth. It may look different for you than it does for others, but in some way or another you've got to be communicating with God. There is no relationship without communication.

I would also like to offer you this caution from Richard Rohr in his book, "Everything Belongs",

...the purpose of the exploration of prayer is not to get anywhere.
We Western people are goal-oriented consumers, and we can't imagine doing anything that won't get us something. But with full deliberation, we need to understand our exploration is not an effort to get anywhere.

I encourage you to consider this truth as it applies not only to prayer, but to all of the disciplines we have discussed.

You will have plenty of opportunities to practice prayer as we move forward. But, perhaps, before we begin to transition to the second part of this book, it would be a good time to pause and pray. Do this however you would like. If you're having trouble getting going, try speaking aloud the following prayer based on Philippians 4.

God – I know I don't have to worry about anything when I offer everything to you. Today I offer you my prayers of anxiety and doubt, but I also offer you words of praise and thanksgiving. I desire _____. I need _____. I am troubled by _____. But I know you are in control of all things, so as I give this all to you, I receive in exchange your peace. Your perfect peace is a greater comfort and protection than anything else in this world. Guard my heart and my mind from this beginning until the end. Amen.

CONCLUSION

Jesus is our ultimate example of a life composed of spiritual disciplines. If we want to get to that place of practicing disciplines, we have to get to him. We also must understand and embrace the greatest act of discipline ever demonstrated in this world - Jesus' willingness to fulfill His father's plans by dying on the cross for us – for you and for me. In Him the great commandment was established by his great commitment. Our ability to love Him and love others was made possible because of His sacrificial love.

Jesus chose us.
And so daily we choose Him,
through the practice of spiritual disciplines.

If, even for a moment, this had felt like a burden to you, I want to gently correct you. Take the weight of the world off of your shoulders and set it back into the hands of God. He wants your complete dependence on him. The beauty of these practices is that they will position us to depend on him more than we depend on ourselves.

Jesus is the sower. The word of God is the seed. The Holy Spirit will instruct us on how to tend our gardens. Practicing the disciplines will simply help us to condition the soil of our souls, so the seeds can grow and bear fruit.

PART II

A Diving Board to Deeper Waters

~Practicing Spiritual Disciplines~

Faith is the eye by which we look to Jesus
A dim-lighted eye is still an eye;
A weeping eye is still an eye.
Faith is the hand with which we lay hold of Jesus
A trembling hand is still a hand.
And he is still a believer whose heart within him
Trembles when he touches the hem of the Savior's garment,
that he may be healed.
Faith is the tongue by which we taste how good the Lord is.
A feverish tongue is nevertheless a tongue,
And even then we may believe, when we are without
the smallest portion of comfort, for our faith is founded
Not on feelings, but upon the promises of God.
faith is the foot by which we go to Jesus
A lame foot is still a foot.
He who comes slowly, nevertheless comes.
~George Mueller

Come weeping.
Come trembling.
Come feverish.
Come lame.
Come slowly.

Whatever condition you find yourself in --
Just come.

This is your place to begin – your diving board. Don't be afraid. The water below is deep, but warm and welcoming. You'll be glad you jumped.

May I offer you one simple suggestion that may make all the difference? Before you turn the page, I want you to do something. Close your eyes. Take a deep breath. Open your hands and rest them on your lap, palms up.

What is about to happen in the time and space you carve out for your relationship with Jesus can go one of two ways. You can hop in the driver's seat, take the wheel and wind up lost and confused; or, you can take the role of passenger, let him drive, and wind up refreshed and refocused. The choice is yours. I can tell you what my default is. It's the one that leaves fingernail marks on my palms. I have to be intentional about the release or I will unknowingly continue with the death grip.

Today you will begin with Day 1. Resist the urge to rush ahead. Take some time to breathe and pray and prepare yourself for what God will do. He *is* going to do something. You can count on that. Give it your all, but also give it time. And don't give up. Sometimes it takes days or weeks or longer, before our hearts and minds settle down enough to hear from him.

You will notice some days include only a simple prompt and a suggestion for engaging in a discipline of abstinence. You may feel like you are not *doing* anything and that is precisely the point. You will be making more room for God to do something instead. Don't skip over these days or try to combine them with more productive endeavors. Let them do their work in you while you cease striving for a bit.

There are a total of 40 days. They are meant to be followed consistently, but not strictly. Don't let too much time pass between your readings, but also let the Spirit guide you into a pace that works best for you. You will get more out of your time if you commit to at least 30 minutes for each reading and response. If you can do 45 minutes to an hour, that's even better. I typically set a timer on my phone so I don't get distracted watching the clock. I also find it helpful to designate a consistent time each day, but you can feel free to do what works best for you. I choose early morning hours for the very reason given by Elisabeth Elliot in her book "Discipline: The Glad Surrender",

--not because I love jumping out of bed, but because it is the only time of day when we can be fairly sure of not being interrupted and because it is best to commune with God before you commune with people. Your attitude toward them will then arise out of your life in Him. Offering to God the first hour of the day is a token of consecration of all of our time.

Whatever you choose, remember – start where you are, use what you have, and do what you can.

Friends, I am on the edge of my seat anticipating the transformation about to take place in your life! As you begin to hear from God, I would love to hear from you. Please keep me posted!

Here we go. On the count of three – eyes closed, deep breath, hands open, palms up.

1 – 2 – 3...

Daily Readings

I realize I can't tell God what to speak, or when to speak it.
But I can position myself in the secret place
so that, when He chooses to speak,
I am found listening.
~Bob Sorge, "Secrets of the Secret Place"

DAY 1 *Water to Wine* by Elizabeth Maxon

Read: John 2:1-11

He didn't use a magic wand.
No spells were cast.
Jesus' presence was enough.

And though the power belonged to Him alone, he invited others in.
He invites us in...
  to be part of the miracle.

A faithful servant carried a pitcher of dirty water to his master, who was expecting wine. Simple obedience in the face of the impossible revealed God's glory and gave birth to faith. It still does today.

In a moment, a miracle can happen.

Water to wine.
Old to new.
Problem to promise.

A traditional Jewish wedding promised to be a joyous occasion with enough food and wine to last for days. Running out of wine would have been a major problem. The promise of a grand celebration would go unfulfilled.

There are gaps that exist between the problems we face and the promises of God. Sometimes they seem impossible to bridge. What will we fill them with?

Anything besides Jesus won't hold up.
Not self-help books.
Not food.
Not drink.
Not TV shows.

Not trips to tropical destinations.
Not the quest for knowledge.
Not even our friends and family.

If the bridge between our problems and God's promises is built with anything else but Him, we will never get to the other side.
We will never experience the transformation from old to new.
We will never taste the fruit of obedience through suffering.
We will never move from a watered down version of life to the rich fullness of who we were created to be.

Jesus' purpose in coming to this world was to lay his life down like a bridge for us to cross - from our problems to His promises.

> *I came that they may have life, and have it abundantly.*
> {John 10:10}

If we invite Jesus into that space between our problems and His promises,
He will fill it with miracles and
He will fill it with meaning.

No magic wands needed.
No book of spells.
The miracles of God are his glory manifested. There is no greater power on heaven or earth.

Capturing the beauty of the conversion of the water into wine, the poet Alexander Pope said,
The conscious water saw its Master and blushed.

Ravi Zacharias goes on to say,
That sublime description could be reworked to explain each miracle. Was it any different in principle for a broken body to mend at the command of its Maker? Was it far-fetched for the Creator of the universe, who fashioned matter out of nothing, to multiply bread for

the crowd? Was it not within the power of the One who called all the molecules into existence to interlock them that they might bear His footsteps?

The same Jesus who turned water to wine, who brought the dead to life, who fed thousands with a meal meant for ten, and walked on water.
That same Jesus wants to bend time and space and matter for you too.

His power at work – *for* you and *in* you.

Whatever problem you are facing today, believe God for a miracle in the gap between that problem and His promises. Invite Him into that space. He won't wedge his way into a gap you're already filling with something else. Give him room.

Walk obediently in the life He has called you to, even when you don't feel like it. Don't let your problem be an excuse for compromising your faithfulness to your God.

Prepare to be transformed. As hard as it may be to believe - there is purpose in the problem. No matter how big or it may be, you can stop searching for answers. Every question can be answered with one name - Jesus.

~ Write down 2 or 3 problems you are facing right now – big or small.
~ Re-read John 2:6-11 {perhaps in another translation this time} and jot down anything significant in your journal.
~ Read one or both of the following passages and reflect on what they mean to you in light of your problems and God's promises today. Jot some more notes in your journal, if you'd like.
Matthew 6:25-33
Romans 8:31-35

The other day I employed the super-holy Bible study method of "open-your-Bible-to-a-random-page-and-choose-the-first-verse-you-see." I landed on a verse beginning with a name I can't even pronounce. This did not seem promising, but I'm glad I hung in there.

Epaphras, who is one of you and a servant of Christ Jesus, sends
greetings. He is always wrestling in prayer for you,
that you may stand firm in all the will of God,
mature and fully assured.
Colossians 4:12

Wrestling in prayer.

I really like this picture of prayer. I think we often talk of prayer as if it's a last resort.

Well, all we can do now is pray.

It seems like this passive, last-ditch effort. We throw a Hail-Mary shot up to heaven (no pun intended) and just wait to see what happens.

But, wrestling. Wrestling is active, fully engaged. It's kind of loud and sweaty. At least it is if you're my kids.

Sometimes prayer is sweet and lovely, hands folded, head bowed, eyes closed, voice hushed. But sometimes it's laid out on the floor, fists pounding, tears flowing, crying out to God. It is confused, angry, hurt, desperate, urgent...*wrestling.*

Sometimes it feels like we're wrestling God Himself, trying to grasp hold of Him and pin Him down. Now, try something: imagine, instead of wrestling *against* God, you're wrestling *alongside* God in prayer.

God is not our opponent. He's certainly not one to be pinned. Perhaps as we struggle, wrestle, through this broken world, it is through prayer that we can find ourselves really experiencing God. We can sense Him wrestling alongside us.

I invite you to wrestle in prayer. Maybe it's for yourself. Maybe it's for your marriage. Maybe it's for your children. Don't just wrestle in your circumstance. Wrestle in prayer. If you can't approach God all pretty and neat and tidy about it – no problem. He never asked us to pray like that.

Even if it feels like you're wrestling against God, that's better than standing at a distance.

When you wrestle, you're close.

God wants us close.

Eventually you'll find, rather than opposing you and trying to pin you down, God has been wrestling alongside you all along.

~ Consider a time when it felt like you were wrestling against God. Perhaps you were trying to convince Him to do something or maybe trying to resist something you felt He was saying or doing. Journal about it.

~ Now, re-frame the experience: wrestling *alongside* God. What difference does this make to you? Jot down the differences in your journal.

~ If you sense God calling you to wrestle alongside Him in prayer about something right now – do it. Get on your knees, close your eyes, and work it out.

DAY 3 *Temptation in Disguise* by Elizabeth Maxon

That's why I'm easy, easy like Sunday morning.

Lionel Richie clearly did not have little kids.
When he sang those lyrics so convincingly, I am quite certain there were no
epic temper tantrums or
marathon whining episodes or
little girl wardrobe malfunctions or
hair pulling or
name calling or
chases of terror
going on at his house.

Have you noticed? Sunday mornings are anything but *easy*.
My version of the song is called '*Crazy*, Like Sunday Morning.'

Our Sunday morning started out smooth enough. I had some time to myself before the kids woke up. They watched a show together on the couch while I made breakfast. Then I began getting us ready for church {insert plot twist}.

Joey was out of town so I was on my own. I should have been able to handle it. It's not like we have 10 kids or anything. There are just two of them, and they are small. Small is manageable, right? Wrong.

I had just turned on the shower when one of them came running down the hall screaming and crying, being chased by the other one who was wielding a wooden spoon and a diabolical laugh. Things had taken a turn. My blood pressure flew up alongside the threats and insults -
I'm never going to play with you ever again!!
I wish I didn't have a brother!
You ALWAYS do that!!
Well, you're a poopy head baby!!

64

That last one is a favorite.

I intervened, they paused, but were back at it again as soon as I turned around.

I redirected, they moved on for a moment, then resumed with increased intensity.

I resorted to threats and insults myself. I started feeling like I might lose my ever loving mind and momentarily considered taking them to church in their pajamas and dropping them off in the kids area for all three services while I went out to a three hour breakfast by myself. But I was afraid someone might call the authorities on me.

The next hour went on like that. Back and forth, spiraling out of control. I was about to blow a gasket when I finally told them, through clinched teeth, to go to their own rooms until they could get it together - until *I* could get it together.

Do you ever have those moments when you stop in the middle of a crazy chaotic home and wonder - *Are we all doomed?*
Have I made some fatal mistake as a parent that has led us to complete relational dysfunction?
Will these children grow up to be mean, spiteful adults who are estranged from their parents?
Is all this anger and ugliness rooted so deep in us that we can never escape it?
Why do other moms seem to be able to handle this stuff so much better than me?
Am I wasting my time trying to fix something that will be eternally broken?
Will I seriously waste hours of my life dealing with this junk?

As I closed each of their bedroom doors to separate us, I began to sense there was more filling the space between us. More than walls and doors. There was something heavy and dark and suddenly all of those frantic questions I had been asking myself became irrelevant because I knew what I was dealing with was far beyond anything I could 'fix'.

When I turned and walked across the hall to my own room I couldn't put my finger on exactly what was going on but I knew what I needed. I bent my knees, took a deep breath, closed my eyes and started the pleading. I lifted the truth up like a banner over that war zone, over all of the injuries and fatalities. Then I went back to blow drying my hair. Life goes on - right in the middle of the battlefield.

When I walked back into the hallway a few minutes later the kids were missing from their rooms. I stood still and quiet, listening for them, holding my breath, hoping no one was in a head lock. That would explain the silence. There was no screaming because there was no breathing!

Just as I set off looking for them I heard talking, not yelling {praise Jesus}, coming from the basement. I went down to find them with the easel paper rolled out on the floor, stickers and markers spread out between them. They were creating their own world. It was a world covered in flowers and sunshine and palm trees and hammocks and rocky roads leading up to picturesque barns. It was a lovely place. They were in a lovely place. Even though we didn't have a lot of time I sat down on the floor and decided to just 'be' in that lovely place with them for a while. Then we left for church. No tears. No tantrums.

I posted a picture on Instagram, giving a brief description of our morning because it had been significant to me. I like to share significant things. But it seemed more significant than several sentences of social media could convey so I kept processing it on the way to church
and as I left the kids in their classroom
and as I joined hundreds of others in collective worship
and then as, amazingly, I listened to my pastor begin preaching, of all things, on the spiritual warfare that is present in the temptations we face in this world.

My whole morning was turning into a living lesson.

At first I didn't identify a clear link between a discussion on temptation and the spiritual war I just endured at home. Then my pastor began listing the top temptations for women. Do you know what they are?

Critical thinking
Jealousy/Envy
Bitterness

Turn back a page and take a look at those questions I was asking myself on a not-so-easy Sunday morning. I think we can check every one of those temptations off the list. I was standing face-to-face with them all.

I tend to think of temptation in more concrete terms. Being tempted in the areas of food or sex or other outwardly obvious behaviors. The above list of temptations is subtler. Those sins are often hidden, not even acknowledged, and yet do untold damage to a person and those around them. If I'm honest, I am tempted in those areas every single day. The enemy of our souls knows our weakness and you can be sure there is strategy involved in the when, where, and how temptation comes exploding into our lives like a grenade.

It wasn't just a home issue we were facing on Sunday. It was a heart issue. What was going on around us was just a symptom of what was going on inside of us. I was being tempted to engage some of my deepest sins. My kids were probably facing theirs too. A problem that deep is above my pay grade, outside my area of expertise.

When a spiritual war is waged, spiritual weapons must be wielded. Over the years I have stockpiled those weapons. They are weapons I am unable to manufacture, but can easily access. They are the words I have read and written and sung and memorized. The truth of them can put any enemy on the ground. I have put myself through boot camp. I have disciplined myself in the ways of prayer and silence and solitude. I know how to take my thoughts captive and interrogate them until I uncover the truth. I'm not particularly strong or tough, but I'm ready. When we are attacked I have the means to fight back. And when a battle is over I get right back to it - the training, the preparation - because a war is being waged for our souls and we can't be caught off guard.

In his book, "The Sacred Romance," John Eldredge says it this way.

He probes the perimeter, looking for a weakness. Here's how this works: Satan will throw a thought or a temptation at us in hopes that we will swallow it. He knows your story, knows what works with you and so the line is tailor-made to your situation...When Satan probes, make no agreement, if something in your heart says, 'Yeah, you're right', then he pours it on.

All those questions I asked myself? They were tailor-made. Yours are too. Far too often I allow them to appear as truth for a moment, maybe longer. That is a dangerous door to open. That is how our perimeter becomes vulnerable to attack. It's a real battle, friends, and nobody can fight alone. We need an army beside us.

My pastor closed his message yesterday by telling us how he and his wife sign off in every note or letter they write to one another.

They don't say 'love you' - although they do.
They don't say 'see ya later' - although they will.
They say what I want to say to you. What I want us to say to each other...

I'm in battle for your soul.

Whose soul are you battling for today? Who is battling for yours?

Because sometimes Sundays are anything but easy. Sometimes the outward struggles are just an indicator of an inward battle. Sometimes our temptations are so hidden that we engage them unknowingly. Sometimes we are losing a war we didn't even know we were fighting. Sometimes we need an army. Let's be that for each other, shall we?

~ What spiritual weapons are you confident you will find in your arsenal? Which ones do you need to stockpile and practice using? What one bit of training could you begin today?

~ Whose soul do you do battle for? Who is doing battle for your soul? If you don't have a community of warriors around you join our 'begin.' community and consider connecting with a begin.buddy. Don't do this alone.

It's difficult for me to get there, to squeeze myself inside that tiny space of here and now. Once I'm there, everything opens up. It's not cramped and tight after all.

In fact, once I get 'in the moment' I must be careful not to look back outside of it. As soon as I do, the pressure builds, the weight increases, my breathing gets shallow, my mind flits all over, and there is unrest.

Rest is found in the moment.

I am showered.
I am dressed.
Make-up on.
Breakfast eaten.
Nothing more required of me – here, now.

Later? Yes. But in this moment I am free.

Free to
Write
Think
Read
Wander
Wonder
Listen

The music in my earbuds picks up pace and pitch. I don't do well with that. Life picks up pace and pitch and I begin to spiral.

How can I keep my pace when the world around me is so unpredictable, so ever-changing? How do I minimize the influence of the frantic and frenzied? How do I keep from absorbing it?

I need breathing room and a chance to remember I can trust Jesus completely.

John 16:32-33 reminds me of Jesus' words,
I've told you all this so that trusting me, you will be unshakable and assured,
deeply at peace. In this godless world you will continue to experience difficulties.
But take heart! I've conquered the world.

The music slows and wraps itself around me. There is complexity, but each instrument works together beautifully. That sound inspires me.

There will be dissonance in life – offensive, disruptive music playing in my ear. I will have to deal with it, but I can also keep seeking a tune to both slow me and move me.

It is the rhythm of grace.

I always find it *in the moment.*

There is a peace. There is a love. You can get lost inside...
~ Needtobreathe, 'Testify'

~ Listen to the song 'Testify' by Needtobreathe. What does it mean to 'get lost inside' the peace, the love, the person of Jesus? How could you start to let go and fall into the moment?
~ Set a timer for at least 15 minutes. Spend it 'in the moment'. Whatever helps you stay present – do that. Close your eyes and breathe deep. Paint a picture. Press and mold a lump of clay. Listen to music. Play music. Meditate on a word or passage. Write about the moment. Sing about the moment. Go for a walk. No pressure. No expectations. No need to produce or perform. Just be in the moment and let the moment hold you.

Dimly Lit by Elizabeth Poplin

Something happened to my very favorite candle.

Actually, something happened to the wick. I've tried everything to revive my blue Volcano candle. I've even googled "how to fix a defective candle wick", but the advice given by the candle wick experts didn't work for my little blue treasure. The flame is so small now, so fragile. Sometimes, from across the room, it looks as if it has finally succumbed to the elements and given up into a puff of smoke. But it never does. It does its job. It burns, but it is dimly lit.

Do you ever feel dimly lit? Barely burning?

Between laundry and errands and the to-do list that only grows longer as motivation and energy grow shorter, we grow weary. We pick up and wipe up and show up and clean up and sometimes want to give up. Between school and emails and schedules and relationships and errands and our attempts to exercise and fulfill every obligation we've signed up for, it's no wonder our candles flicker. It's no wonder, on some days, your flame is faint. It seems like the slightest wind - just one more thing - could completely do you in.

One of my favorite verses in the Bible says this.
> *A bruised reed He will not break,*
> *and a dimly burning wick He will not extinguish.*
> Isaiah 42:3

I love that the Lord, in his tenderness for you, knows that on many days you feel dimly lit. Not good enough. Not pretty enough. Not together enough. And sometimes, just plain tired.

I want you to imagine God lovingly cupping His tender hands around your dimly lit flame. Imagine Him scooping you up in His lap to hold you for a while. Imagine Him breathing life and breath back into what's left of you at the end of the day. He sees every loving thing you've done. He knows every hurt you've healed. He hears every quick prayer you've prayed. He witnesses every smile you force. He delights over every joy you've experienced. He walks beside you every step. And He loves you more than you can comprehend. Take that in.

He loves you more than you can comprehend.

When you feel dimly lit, know that God's word says He will not extinguish your flame. He treasures it. He sees it, sees you, as beautiful. He longs to take it and cup it and restore it to wholeness and joy. To peace and purpose. To rest and redemption.

On the many days that my flame is dimly lit, the only true remedy I've found is Jesus. He is the cure for the dimly lit life. He is the revival for the tired spirit. He is the best friend for the lonely heart.

When your flame is barely burning, find Him. Sit with Him. Grab a blanket and your Bible and tell Him you need Him. He waits for the chance to love you. To cup your little flame in His hands and keep it safe and burning. With him there is peace and purpose. Clarity for chaos. Strength for weariness. Deep breaths for tattered, teary ones.

There's no stronger shelter for dimly lit flames than the presence of Jesus. So press on, beautiful one, and let your little light so shine, even when it flickers.

Your dimly lit days are His specialty.

~ Close your eyes and imagine God's hands carefully cupped around your dimly lit life. Pour out your needs to him and then...listen.
~ Read Isaiah 42:3 in various translations. Respond to the verse and your time with God in your journal.

DAY 6 *Finders Keepers* by Elizabeth Maxon

Sometimes I rely more on the ritual than the relationship.
Rituals can be a good thing. But...

Rituals don't care when you are hurting and struggling. Relationships do.
Rituals don't get all up in your business. Relationships do.
Rituals don't surprise you by meeting you in unexpected ways. Relationships do.

Jesus is a person. People connect through relationships - not rituals.

In my relationship with Jesus I so often do all the talking.
Blah Blah Blah Blah
I am a master at praying and laying my life down at the throne of God, but I have a tendency to stand from my knees too soon and walk away before I hear what he has to say in response. Relationships require listening and finding out what the other person has to say on the matter. I am always rewarded for my listening. Maybe not immediately, but always.

Sometimes it takes only one moment.
Only one verse.

~ ~ ~

It was an ordinary fall night, right in the middle of back-to-school stuff. The pace of life was moving fast, and I was feeling the effects. As I drowsily reached for the kitchen light before going to bed, something stopped me. That book of truth sat still under a pile of bills and lists and advertisements on the counter, but I heard it whisper to me. There can be so much drowning noise in my head, but that night I could hear.
I pushed the pile aside. I opened those pages wearily, and then it was me - torn open.
I was ready to listen, ready to find - and be found.

In an instant, a few words spoke to me. I felt the need to dig deeper, because a simple verse is never just a simple verse. I began reading other translations and commentaries and eventually stumbled upon something.

You crown the year with your bounty;
your wagon tracks overflow with abundance.
{Psalm 65:11 ESV}

You crown the year with your goodness; your footsteps drop
prosperity behind them. {Psalm 65:11 ISV}

The wagon tracks. The foot paths.
What happens when a wagon rides over and over the same track?
What happens when someone treads over and over the same path?

The ground becomes hard and bare.

You crown the year with a bountiful harvest; even the hard
pathways overflow with abundance. {Psalm 65:11 NLT}

The hard pathways.

And yet even the most deeply worn tracks, the hardest of pathways, produce abundance and prosperity in the presence of the one who brings life and growth in the hard places.

The suffering, the grieving, the frustration, and the disappointment are heavy to bear. They pack us down, leaving us dry and cracked, unable to produce anything good. And yet the feet of God fall softly on that dirty, worn track of our lives and something beautiful begins to grow in their wake.

His presence is all we need for life to sprout up - lush and new.

You crown the year with your goodness; and richness overflows
wherever you are. {Psalm 65:11 GW}

When he comes, so does new life.

What if we made it a priority to step into his presence, to step into
new life?
Imagine how far that one step could take us. Imagine what we might
find there.

~~~

Years ago I let my mind wander to this place and I began a year full
of 'First Friday Finds'.

On the first Friday of every month I invited others to join me as I
took a few moments to find what our hearts really need - the grace
words of our Savior. The goal was simply to open the word of God
and let it speak to us. These were the parameters {because
parameters make me feel safe and help me focus}.
{1} Open your Bible {or turn it on}.

{2} Find ONE verse. You can randomly choose. You can search for
a keyword. You can flip to a particular chapter. You can go back to
something were recently intrigued by. Take a breath, allow yourself
to be guided to that spot, and then see what you find. This isn't the
time to go back to an old favorite. It's time to discover something
new.

{3} Read your verse. Read it again. And again. Look at it in various
translations. Read 2 or 3 verses surrounding it if you need some
context. As you read, don't be too focused on how you can say
something profound about the verse, but instead allow the verse to
say something profound to you. Even if it's slow going at first, give
it some time.

{4} 15 minutes flat. Set your timer. After you've taken a little time
to let the words settle into your spirit take 15 minutes to record what

you've found. If you have trouble coming up with anything, just copy the verse. Underline words or phrases that resonate with you. Write something about that word or phrase. Remember you are not being graded and there is no 'right' or 'wrong'. Stick to your time limit because if you feel the need to do more you may not do it at all, and that would be a shame.

We will incorporate this practice into our readings occasionally. You can feel free to try it more often if you'd like. We won't call them First Friday Finds because you may not do them on first Fridays - or on Friday at all. Instead we will call them 'Finders Keepers'. When you uncover hidden treasures of scripture and take your time to record a response, something happens. Those treasures become yours. They are tucked away inside of you forever.

Today is your first 'Finders Keepers'. Find a verse. Or choose one from the list below.
~ 1 Corinthians 16:13
~ Romans 14:23
~ John 15:5
~ 2 Chronicles 20:12
Follow the above steps and see where they take you.

DAY 7 *Stop The Madness* by Elizabeth Maxon

I envy people who are not crazy. I'm being serious.

I have a handful of friends who had pretty normal childhoods, stable families, loyal friends, nothing traumatic or wild to report other than the time their second-cousin-once-removed showed up at the family reunion drunk. I know their lives are not perfect, but their course in life has never deviated too far. These are the people I try to channel when I feel like I am going to completely lose it and go ballistic on someone.

I know that thought would never cross the mind of a non-crazy person. I have crazy in me. I routinely feel like I might literally come out of my skin. I harbor tension that makes my jaw clench as I sleep, which seems to only be relieved by either screaming at the top of my lungs, throwing something, or sobbing uncontrollably. I am keenly aware that 'losing your mind' isn't just something people say but something that really happens. I misplace mine on a regular basis. I could go on, but I think you get the idea.

My crazy usually lies hidden behind the social graces every good southern girl has been taught, or sits cowering under the commands of my highly trained behavior modification skills, but eventually it pokes its ugly head out and starts causing problems.

Being crazy isn't easy {especially for my kids and husband, I'm guessing - poor things}. But lately I've been thinking my crazy may actually be evidence of God's mercy.

Every time I think I might have a handle on this life, the craziness seems to get a hold of me and I am reminded how foolish I have been in all my independent acting and thinking and feeling.

I am the vine; you are the branches. Whoever abides in me and I in him, he will bear much fruit;

APART FROM ME YOU CAN DO NOTHING.
~ Jesus {John 15:5}

In case you didn't guess, the caps were mine. Sometimes I need Jesus to raise his voice with me.

When I feel crazy my mind starts spinning and
I need answers
and a solution
and something to stop the voices in my head!

At some point I eventually end up in the same place – desperately asking God for help with all it. And it doesn't help. Then I start to think my mind is so full of nonsense that I can't even properly ask the Lord of all creation for what I need, because surely he could set things right if I just asked the right questions and got the right answers. I wear myself out with all this business of asking and not getting answers until I am so weary and frazzled I finally crawl up on His lap and let myself fall into Him.

And the craziness lifts.
And that verse proves true.

Stop asking and start abiding.

Don't let yourself get so far away from the source of truth that all you can hear are lies. Don't believe you should be able to handle anything when what you really need is to take your hands off of it and be held.

Oh God, that my being would literally be an extension of your being. That you would fuse my spirit back onto yours so there is not a breath of space between us. No room for crazy to creep in and take back over.

That this dead branch of a life would be reconnected to its vine and receive all the nourishment needed to produce something ripe and sweet in this world.
Oh God, apart from you I can do nothing. Why do I ever try?

~ Pray this prayer aloud to God or write your own.
~ Read John 15. Respond in your journal.

DAY 8 *Letting Go* by Breann Griffin Nicholson

Knocked down.

It's an experience we've all had. Whether it's a child falling on the playground or an adult, being hit by worry, grief, or fear.

No matter how hard we get knocked down, we can always get back up with help from Jesus. If you have a hard time believing that, I understand. There was a time when I did too.

One thing knocks me down more than anything else – worry. Friends, I am a world-class worrier. There, I said it.

I overthink situations. I stress out over everything. I worry about way too many things, way too much of the time. Maybe you do too. Worry poisons most of our lives on a daily basis. We think it is inevitable, unavoidable. Let me give you a little glimpse into how worry has impacted my journey.

It all began with a traumatic hit to my head. The doctor diagnosed it as a concussion. The intense anxiety started soon after and I was led into a world of doubt, fear and uncertainty. Over the next two years, my struggles included being homebound from the university I was attending, panic attacks that filled my body with pain and fear, and doubt about where God was leading me. I was frustrated. I was angry. I was in a place I never planned to be in.
But that's the thing - our plans don't always match up with the story God is writing with our lives.

Where did my story lead? Not where I expected.

It led to that season of struggle but it also led to a quaint dinner out with a group of ladies right in the middle of that struggle. After the small talk was over and our meals were half eaten the conversation began to run deeper. The next thing I knew I was in tears and the words of my story were being told aloud for the first time. That night God told me to share. His presence was in the room making that possible. I felt such a freedom.

That struggle led to that dinner and that dinner led to my involvement in a summer bible study. Not only did I participate but God called me to serve and lead other women. It was something I hadn't planned on but God was writing that chapter into my story.

I was reminded many times over the summer that God's plan and His timing for me are perfect. I was also reminded that it is my responsibility to choose joy, even when it's hard. But it got easier and easier as I let him do the leading.

That summer I let go, and let God. I let God completely control my path. I opened my hands to Him and let Him guide me. The result has been amazing! He has led me to a better understanding of my purpose, my calling and my role as His child. I keep joy in front of me and worry behind me.

Sometimes letting go is scary because you are afraid of falling, of being knocked down. But if you are in the arms of Jesus – you will always be lifted up.

I have learned that *worry does not have to be inevitable.* God tells us this truth in His Word.

Come to me, all you who are weary and burdened, and I will give you rest.
Take my yoke upon you and learn from me, for I am gentle and humble in heart, and you will find rest for your souls.
For my yoke is easy and my burden is light
Matthew 11:28-30

By the power of God's presence and promises, I am determined to not be a worrier. Instead I am a listener, a follower, an open-handed child.

Through the struggles and the pain, I have heard God whisper to me - *Here I am, child. Look to me. I have a plan much greater than you can ever imagine. Place your worry on my shoulders and let me give you peace and joy.*

Maybe you are on the ground right now and feel like you may never get back up. Maybe you feel broken, unloved, or worried. I know that place. I have been there. But being knocked down is what taught me that whole-heartedly depending on God is the only way to find true joy and freedom.

Because of HIM the joy can be recovered.
Because of HIM the freedom can be found.
Because of HIM the fighting can end.

We aren't facing these mountains alone. It's time to open our hearts, open our hands and let go. *Let God.*

Stay joyful, friends.

~ As you come to God today, physically open your hands and offer up everything you are holding onto.
~ In your journal make a list of all the things in your life causing worry and unrest right now. Read Philippians 4:6-7 and Psalm 55:22. How do you sense God responding to your worries? Journal about it.

Imagine having a death sentence at birth.

Despite that, he was hidden as an infant, floated down the Nile River in a basket, adopted by royalty, raised as the son of the most powerful man in the world, and forced to flee to the desert because of an act of violence. He lived a relatively uneventful life out in the wilderness for 40 years, encountered God in a burning bush, and, well, you can read the other details for yourself.

Not to give the whole story away, but this man wound up rescuing a nation from slavery. Ultimately, he was used by God to save the people of God. Pretty amazing for a guy who may not have even known much of anything about God until he was old and that whole bush incident happened.

The story of Moses has always intrigued me. Someone initially oblivious and later reluctant in his pursuit of the calling of God. Despite all the obstacles, and perhaps because of them, Moses ultimately allowed God to fulfill a great purpose in his life.

Every night I pray for God to fulfill a great purpose in the lives of my kids.
Every morning I ask God to take my life and use it for His purposes too.

For me, my faith has always had a lot to do with the plans of God and how I fit into those. There is something both exciting and comforting about playing a supporting role in the greatest story ever told. {And by the way - realizing you're not the playwright *or* the leading role is key to a happy ending.}

A few years ago I was struck by something my friend and pastor, Chris Payne said,
God had Moses in Midian {the desert} because of his future, not

because of his past.

As Moses sat by that well in that dusty desert town after running for his life from Egypt, he may have felt like he had hit rock bottom. He may have even felt like he was living some kind of cruel punishment. His own people had rejected him. His adoptive family and the culture he had grown up in rejected him. Moses didn't have anyone he could identify with. He had no place to belong. The future probably looked grim and hopeless. He may have considered his past and how it ultimately led him to what seemed like a dead end. In that moment it may have been difficult for Moses to look ahead, much less *move* ahead.

Have you ever felt that way?

Have your past decisions or experiences led you to a place that feels like the end? Do you look back and consider that you are in this pit of a place because of your past?

But what if you're not in your current situation simply as a result of your past,
but as preparation for your future.

The Moses who tucked tail and ran in Exodus 2 wasn't ready to be the Moses who saved a nation in Exodus 14. Sometimes, like Moses, we run away from what we thought was our destiny, because it didn't work out the way we planned. Or maybe we feel like we just missed it all together. Messed the whole thing up. Or maybe we feel like it was taken from us. We got gypped.

But *maybe* God's destiny for us is something different. Maye it is something greater. Maybe all we've walked through has been preparing us for that time, that place, that *purpose.*

If you're still alive on this earth God has a purpose for you.
    Are your eyes looking ahead at the future he is calling you to or

are you turned around backwards mourning what was, or what could have been?

Are you worried your best days are behind you or do you trust God to use what's behind to prepare you for what's ahead?

Shifting your gaze from past to future can mean exchanging despair for hope,
failure for freedom,
your small story for His big one.

What does my future hold?

It's a question I've asked a thousand times.
I don't have all the answers but I do know one thing for sure –

God will take everything that has led me to today,
and use it to propel me into tomorrow,
with a purpose.

~ What parts of your past have you allowed to hold you back? In what ways might God want to take what has been to lead you to what will be? In what ways have you already seen him do this in your lives or the lives of others?

~ Spend some time exploring part of Moses' story in Exodus 2. Record anything significant God reveals to and how it might pertain to your life.

DAY 10 *Desert Wanderings* by Elizabeth Maxon

Read Matthew 4:1-11.

Ever wandered through the desert?
It can be so lovely getting lost in among the cactus and tumbleweed, finding wildflowers, and watching the sun set behind giant red rocks. I lived in Arizona for almost seven years. I found surprising beauty in the desert. But...
there was also heat
and snakes
and coyotes
and scorpions
and dust storms
and dry, cracked earth.

It's one thing to spend an afternoon discovering desert beauty and it's another thing to spend days there alone and without food.
Not so lovely.
But that's what Jesus did.
40 days.
40 nights.
Alone.
No food.

And then the enemy showed up with one purpose - to tempt him.

Jesus allowed himself to become vulnerable and weak not because he wanted to, not because he was forced to, but because he was <u>led</u> to that desert place.

Then Jesus was led up by the Spirit into the wilderness...

No one ever wants to find themselves feeling alone, weak, tired, hungry, and vulnerable.
But sometimes we are led to that place, to that desert season in our

lives.

When we are at our weakest and most vulnerable, when we are just plain tired of the daily struggles of life or the crises that just won't stop running us over,
the world tempts us.

We are offered all kinds of shiny things promising to
'make life better'
or 'ease the pain'
or 'give us what we deserve'.

In the middle of the desert we can become so preoccupied with our own well-being and what is best for ourselves that we accept those offers which ultimately are just a mirage. We are so exhausted and disoriented, we believe we are moving towards a pool of water offering refreshment and fulfillment to our dry souls, but it turns out to just be more sand, more desert we can't escape.

Jesus knew there was only one way to escape the temptations in the desert. There was one way for Him and one way for us -
the word of God.

Jesus is alone and vulnerable in the desert when Satan tempts him to use his power to turn stones into bread and stop his hunger, but Jesus answers,
It is written - man shall not live by bread alone, but by every word that comes from the mouth of God.

Satan then tempts Jesus to demonstrate his authority by calling upon angels to do his bidding but Jesus answers,
It is written - you shall not put the Lord your God to the test.

And still Satan would not relent. He tempts Jesus to gain more power by declaring his allegiance to the devil and receiving authority over all the kingdoms of the world but Jesus answers,

It is written - you shall worship the Lord your God and him only shall you serve.

And then - the devil left. The temptation subsided and the scriptures tell us
···*angels came and were ministering to him.*

In the desert season Jesus didn't succumb to the temptations of temporary pleasure, temporary relief of discomfort.   Jesus remembered the eternal truth of God.

It wasn't about a little story he was living in the moment.   It was about a much bigger story God has been writing since the beginning of time.
And every. single. thing. the enemy offers, the world offers, pales in comparison to what God offers.   If you know God's word, you know that's true.

If the greatest way to survive a desert season is to proclaim and stand upon what has been written by God, then I guess we better darn well know what is written.

There is no substitute for studying God's word.
There is no better way to safeguard yourself for the desert wandering to come.
There is no other way to ensure that even in the driest of seasons you will still grow and flourish.

When we commit ourselves to knowing the word of God we don't have to completely avoid temptation. We don't have to run scared from it. We can actually face it, and overcome it. One sweet victory after another.

Knowing what is written is knowing the greater story.
It's not just knowing bits and pieces of scripture and trying to make them fit into our little lives but knowing the depth and breadth of

God's story and how you fit into it. Because you do. You fit. Of course you don't look the same as those church-y, holy roller people. Have you ever seen a puzzle made up of hundreds of identical pieces? It is your unique lines and angles that allow you to be a part of something bigger than yourself.

When you know God's word you know this -
what Satan was offering Jesus,
what he offers us,
is all just a <u>trick.</u>
God has already given us everything. There is nothing we need that he withholds from us. To submit to the enemy's ways is pointless because there is nothing of value he can offer us that Jesus hasn't already died and bought for us on the cross.

The only way to live a truly abundant life is to live it within the pages penned by the Great Author, the one who wrote you into existence and who writes you into eternity.

And the only way to live that story is to know it.

The more we understand his story, the more we understand our own.

Believe me, I have chased after my fair share of mirages in this life but I have learned the truth...
when our roots are connected to streams of living water,
there is no desert season we cannot survive.

~ What temptations are you facing? What dry, desert season is wearing you down? Fill in the blanks and allow God's word the power over your situation.
I keep falling into the trap of believing _____,
but *it is written* _____.
Copy down that statement and a corresponding passage of scripture on an index card. Keep it by your bed to make it your First-Last thought. Seal your days with the truth.

Today is your second 'Finders Keepers'.

{1} Open your Bible {or turn it on}.

{2} Find your verse. You can randomly choose. You can search for a keyword. You can flip to a particular chapter. You can go back to something you were recently intrigued by.

Or choose one from the list below:

~ Hebrews 10:35
~ 1 Corinthians 16:13
~ Romans 14:23
~ John 15:5
~ 2 Chronicles 20:12

Take a breath, allow yourself to be guided to that spot, and then see what you find. This isn't the time to go back to an old favorite. It's time to discover something new.

{3} Read your verse. Read it again. And again. Look at it in various translations. Read 2 or 3 verses surrounding it if you need some context. As you read, don't be too focused on how you can say something profound about the verse, but instead allow the verse to say something profound to you. Even if it's slow going at first, give it some time.

{4} 15 minutes flat. Set your timer. After you've taken a little time to let the words settle into your spirit take 15 minutes to record what you've found. If you have trouble coming up with anything, just copy the verse. Underline words or phrases that resonate with you. Write something about that word or phrase. Remember you are not being graded and there is no 'right' or 'wrong'. Stick to your time limit because if you feel the need to do more you may not do it at all, and that would be a shame.

When I don't spend time in God's word, I'm not the only one who suffers.

I had just finished leading a Bible study for young moms as the holidays were approaching. With school activities, Thanksgivings feasts, Christmas shopping and church events, my time with the Lord pretty much came to a screeching halt. I sensed the lack of fruit in my life and how it was affecting me as a wife and a mom but it wasn't enough to motivate me to wake up 30 minutes earlier in the morning to spend time with Him.

I told myself I would resume my quiet time and get back into His word after the craziness of life settled down. After all, I had 30 treat bags to make look like reindeers and I refused to have one more Pinterest Fail at school!

In the middle of a hectic schedule we experienced some trials in our extended family. It was something we had never navigated before. The next thing I knew my marriage was suffering. I found myself getting very bitter and upset that my husband wouldn't handle things the way I wanted him to. Yes, I know. He is the leader of our home. But I would like him to lead more the way I want him to lead. Uh-oh. Bad place to be.

One night it all came to a head when my husband chose not to deal with a family member who really hurt my feelings. His lack of action hurt me deeply, and I made sure to let him know that loud and clear.

It happened to be a Monday night. Monday night is supposed to be family night. Monday night is supposed to be the night we drop off our little girl at dance class and walk over to Starbucks with our two-year-old little man, share a coffee, and just relax. But not this night. Nope. That wasn't going to happen.

In the time I took to let him know how upset I was, I made us late. I found myself hurriedly shoving a tutu on my little girl as my husband walked upstairs to our office. When I told him we were ready to go he said he would just meet us there because he had a deadline he needed to meet in the next 30 minutes.

That was the straw for me. Family night was ruined and I was furious. Too much tension and bitterness had ruined everything.

When we got home I whipped up some cheese eggs for the kids and took my scowling face upstairs. I was so angry. My heart was hard and I felt trapped in a web of sin I had created myself. I felt so stuck.

It had been weeks since I had spent time with the Lord and it seemed the longer I went without seeking him the more I didn't WANT to. The guilt of avoiding him and thinking I could handle things myself was turning me even further away from Him. Things had spiraled out of control.

In desperation I grabbed my Bible and just opened it. There it was - Psalm 119. My eyes instantly went to a scripture I had underlined.

My flesh trembles in fear of you; I stand in awe of your laws.
Psalm 119:120

In the margin I had previously drawn an arrow specifically to that verse and noted "read with a heart of repentance."

I broke down. The walls of my hardened heart came down too. The Lord used his truth to crack the surface that night. I was reminded that my flesh literally does tremble in fear of Him. He is the Sovereign God who saved me, bestows grace upon me, and calls me out when I'm out of order. He's the captain of this ship, not me.

In the middle of all of the tears I simply whispered, "I want you to win in this situation Lord."

I turned to Hebrews 11:6.

And without faith it is impossible to please God,
because anyone who comes to him must believe
that he exists and that he rewards those who earnestly seek him.

Rewards those who earnestly seek Him.

Right then I knew that as much as I was kicking and screaming and fighting God, my heart truly wanted God to intervene. I wanted God to win in this, in my marriage, in my parenting, in my extended family. I had been fighting a losing battle without him. The very fact that I wanted Him to win was a reminder to my heart that I was earnestly seeking Him. It was that simple. It was all He required. I believe He rewards us when we earnestly seek Him.

His reward in this situation was grace. He used it to make my heart palatable again. I was positioned for humility and I would need to go to my husband and apologize for being his crazy-town wife who wasn't trusting his leadership. We had gotten to that place all because I wasn't making my time with the Lord a priority. I had nothing good to offer my people because I hadn't allowed him to offer anything good to me.

My goodness towards others is the direct result of his goodness towards me. So earnestly, I seek him.

~ Look up the word 'earnest'. Look up the word 'seek'. Write down their meaning in your journal.
~ Pray this simple prayer to God – *Earnestly I seek you.*
~ In the scriptures what does it say will happen when we seek God. Write down a list of all the results of seeking God. {hint: Deuteronomy 4:29, Psalm 34:10, Proverbs 8:17, Jeremiah 29:12-14; Matthew 6:33; Matthew 7:7-8...there's more too :)} Choose a verse about seeking and make a 'First-Last Thought' to add to your collection.

Sometimes I get this uncomfortable claustrophobic feeling.

I'm not talking about that time when I started shaking uncontrollably inside the MRI machine and they had to pull me out. That *was* a nightmare though. Seriously. How can you keep from losing your ever-loving mind when you are cramped in a dark tunnel with a metal mask on your face and a loud hammering sound coming at you from all sides? I marched my freaking-out self right through those double doors and never looked back.

This feeling. It's sort of like that. But it's different.

Sometimes I feel like the world is so full that I have to elbow my way through the crowd. It's slow moving and I can't settle into a brisk pace. Sometimes I can't move forward at all. There are moments when I even feel myself being pushed down by the masses. I start stumbling backwards. Suddenly I can't even see where it was I was heading.

I look around at all the people and what they are successfully doing
and how many thousands of people follow them on twitter
and how well-organized their websites are
and how many well-known figures endorse their books
and how perfectly artsy all their Instagram pictures are
and how hilariously witty all their Facebook posts are
and I feel myself hyperventilating.

I think I might just get swallowed up by the masses.
I get that freaking-out feeling again.
I'm afraid I will disappear and nobody will even know I was there.
In the crowd.
I want to start pushing people away from me. I want my space. And I don't want it to be cyberspace. I want it to be a space filled with fresh air I can really breath and grass I can really sink my feet into. I

95

want it to be big enough for me to run and run and run. Away from the crowd.

Social media and the internet can make me feel claustrophobic.

I know there is so much value to these tools. Really, I do. But there are seasons in our lives when the cost outweighs the benefit.

I am a wife, a mother, a writer, a speaker, a reader, a runner, a friend, a counselor, an artist, and so much more.

I don't have time to manage social media. There is so much living I want to do and so much dying that happens every time I chase a rabbit hole into my phone.

Is it possible we are becoming too 'connected'? With every connection I make I feel the responsibility of that one and then the pressure to make another one and another one... It never ends.

I feel quality suffering for quantity.

Our culture certainly has a tendency to value more, more, more. I feel that happening with technology. I wonder how it will affect my kids. I wonder how it is affecting me and my marriage and my friendships {the real ones}.

I may have more questions than answers, but I believe we need to keep asking them. One thing I know for sure is there are times we need to remove ourselves from the crowded arena and take a detour down a quiet dirt road in the country somewhere.

If you've been feeling that claustrophobic feeling maybe it's time to step away from the crowd. Maybe you should take a trip to the biggest field you can find, and run. Run and run and run - wild and free. And then allow for some space between you and cyberspace. No Facebook. No Twitter. No Instagram. No Snapchat. No surfing the web for ideas, inspiration, and inspiration. There is a greater source for all those things and we need to get back to it.

~ Try a social media fast. Designate a certain number of days or weeks you will abstain from it. Or determine certain times of day you will not allow yourself access to your phone and/or computer. Set alarms and passwords if necessary. It's time to remind your phone who is boss. Before you make a plan, say a prayer. Ask for God's wisdom so that you can make the *best* decision for you and your people {not the easy one}.

The Girl at Starbucks by Elizabeth Maxon

Do not spoil what you have by desiring what you have not;
but remember what you now have was once among the things you
hoped for.
~Epicuris

Her freckled face was framed with curly red hair. I noticed because as she walked past me her neck turned to allow her a longer look. I lifted my head and smiled. Her half-smile broke open wide and her eyes seemed to gaze longingly, taking in the whole scene of me.

It sounds strange, I know. To think that a pre-teen girl following her father into Starbucks would long for my life. A life of juggling motherhood and sick children and work and writing and the schedule that comes along with a busy family of four. Maybe my hair was standing straight up or I had egg on my face. Or maybe it really was a longing look.

I considered what that gangly young girl may have seen on that shaded sidewalk this morning...
a grown up girl
not dependent on her dad for a ride
doing as she pleases
drinking what she wants
reading what she loves
free to make her own choices

It wasn't all that long ago that I was her - the girl with the longing eyes.
As a 5th grader I remember seeing my favorite Sunday school teacher that way. She was a beautiful young woman who held a freedom that split the world wide open in front of her like the sweetest summer watermelon.

I imagined how that freedom could take me all the places and show me all the things and teach me all the lessons that I chose - instead of the ones chosen for me. But we don't acquire freedom all at once like we acquire a driver's license.

Bit by bit we receive it.

And if we're not careful -

bit by bit we release it.

This morning's temperature was cooler than it should have been, like some leftover spring breeze found its way out from under the thick summer air. My kids were in Vacation Bible School and all my meetings got cancelled. I found myself sharing a table with a decaf hazelnut Americano, my laptop, and a pile of books. My 'Bach station' on Pandora was feeding an airy instrumental version of 'Be Thou My Vision' into my ears as I recalled the poetic words I know by heart.

In that moment the obstacles I faced faded, and the sweet freedom I possess resurfaced.

I felt the chains falling off. The ones I unknowingly wrap around my own wrists and ankles on a regular basis.

We live our childhood anticipating the days of freedom that lie ahead and then as soon as we get there we begin finding ways to enslave ourselves all over again.

Shame

Guilt

Comparison

Perfectionism

Greed

Fear

Discontentment

The general rat race of life.

When we let the world define the vision for our life we hand our freedom over.

I've done that. I do that.

And then I wind up feeling like I'm living in a dark and dirty jail cell. Depressing.

I have felt depressed.

On that particular day I looked down and saw the key in my hand. It had been there all along.

Sometimes I let the freedom I carry point me towards all the decisions that need to be made and questions that need to be answered. Suddenly freedom feels more like slavery. If I'm not careful I lose sight of God's vision for my life and bind myself up in all sorts of unrealistic worldly expectations.

And then someone walks by with longing eyes and I am reminded that I stand holding a life that was the dream of a younger me. Instead of trying to survive it, I will treasure it.

Yes - life is hard,
but we are free.

Sometimes it helps to step outside of our messy lives and see who we are with fresh eyes, with the eyes of our younger freedom-seeking selves. To be reminded that not only have we been given a vision but *we are a vision.*

The hands that knit you together, the mouth the breathed life into your lungs - behind them is a God who had a vision for something wonderful...you.

And He certainly doesn't want you wasting all that wonderful-ness locked up in the dark. Today let's quietly recommit ourselves to living as the wonderful visions He created us to be and using every bit of our freedom to make our vision Him.

Be Thou my vision, oh Lord of my heart
Naught be all else to me, save that Thou art
Thou my best thought by day or by night
Waking or sleeping, Thy presence my light...

...Thou and Thou only first in my heart
High King of Heaven, my treasure Thou art

~ Think back to your childhood. What did you once dream of doing or being when you were younger? Have any of those dreams become a reality? Do you appreciate them or ignore them?

~ Listen to the song 'Be Thou My Vision'. As you do, close your eyes and concentrate on the words. Make them a prayer to God. Write any of your own thoughts or feelings about the 'vision of your life' and 'being the vision of God' in your journal.

DAY 15 *Help Me Pray* by Kai A. Pineda

"No one can make you inferior without your consent!"
- Eleanor Roosevelt

I don't know if you have ever felt this way, but I have to admit, over the past few months Instagram has caused me to question my dedication to studying the Word of God. I know. I should not be comparing myself to anyone else as this leads one down a horrible path of shame and guilt. But when I see these beautiful pictures of bibles placed ever so perfectly beside gorgeous calligraphy notes it becomes a bit intimidating.

I wonder if you have ever compared your walk with God to a stranger on social media who seems to be the perfect poster child for the best Christian ever? If so, then let me tell you, you are not alone. You would think I could never feel inferior since I am a pastor whose life is studying the Word of God and sharing it with others. But I do. I have. And I did!

Over the last year, I have been asking God to take me deeper. Most people see me as dedicated and disciplined but I could feel something was missing. I was not sure what is was, but the relationship I hold dear with God started to change and I could see myself moving away from disciplines without understanding why.

I would be scrolling through my timeline on Facebook or gazing at the pictures on Instagram and find myself wondering why I wasn't producing or growing the way I imagined the women on the other end of my computer were. I had no idea of her struggles or even what could be going on in her life, but the illustrations she shared daily caused me to feel 'less than' and I started to question myself. Was studying for weekly messages enough? What could I do to jumpstart a passion that seemed to be waning? Was I really who I thought I was, or had I lost parts of her along the way?

The questions spun around in my mind for a long time. I thought: Maybe I need a new bible. Maybe one I could color. Maybe I need to create a daily schedule to keep me committed and hit every target, every day. Or maybe I should fast more and let go of some things so I can get back to the place I thought God wanted me.

I will tell you this. I did not get the new Bible, trying to be perfect was a big fail, and trying to get back to a place was not what God wanted. What I did do, was fast. And in fasting I realized what was missing had nothing to do with studying, but everything to do with my prayer life.

I was startled at the revelation. I had a flashback of a time in my life when prayer was not a routine, but prayer was something I did all day, every day. When God would prompt me, I would draw myself into prayer no matter where I was or who I was with. Somehow I had stopped this way of life and started to make prayer a specific time. It began slowly over the years as I saw others doing it and thought maybe this is the way I should pray. I let go of something special God had taught me early in my walk with Him and it was leaving me empty. I tried to follow a pattern that was not how God desired us to pray in 1 Thessalonians 5:16-18 (NIV)

Rejoice always, pray continually, give thanks in all circumstances; for this is God's will for you in Christ Jesus.

In the Greek the phrase "pray continually" is the word adialeíptōs which means "nothing left between" or "without any unnecessary interval (time-gap)".

See, prayer is not to be scheduled but to be lived out daily as you wake-up, move about, and go through your day. You are to leave nothing unspoken and let no manner of time keep you from speaking to your Father in heaven. This reality takes away so much of the stress I think a lot of us put on ourselves about prayer. Now don't get me wrong, as you set aside a time to study the Word you need to pray first so the Holy Spirit can guide you as you study. In the morning, wake up and talk to your Father, but don't just leave it there. Prayer is a life of devotion, not a moment of dedication.

When God reminded me of this beautiful daily encounter He carves out for His children, I understood the tension I had been feeling. Now I could scroll through posts and timelines and embrace what others were doing. I could rejoice with them instead of feeling inferior to them. I could celebrate their lives and let the comparisons go. The awakening of my heart again to pray like the Word instructs in 1 Thessalonians 5, gives me reason to rejoice and give thanks. When we pray continually we can face whatever comes our way looking through the eyes of Christ.

My prayer for you is this - take a moment and ask God to teach you to pray continually. Let this become a way of life you adopt. It is what our Savior Jesus did as He walked the earth. This beautiful way of prayer will deepen your relationship with the Father and cause you to be a place of hope and love for others. Your devotion will deepen and out of it will flow compassion, not comparisons.

~ What would it look like to pray continually? Jot down some of the main things on your schedule for the next few days and consider what it would look like to be praying through all of that. Consider setting an alarm on your phone 2-3 times over the course of today as 'prayer pauses'. Use those reminders to get you in the habit of being in constant communication with your Father in heaven.

I love bagels.
And pasta.
And fresh-baked bread with butter melting on it.
Is your mouth watering yet?

I remember the first time a friend told me she had gone over to the dark side. You know what I'm talking about - gluten-free {gasp!}.

On more than one occasion I said to myself - I could NEVER do that.

I was eating bagels almost every morning.
I was cooking pasta at least a couple of times a week.
My trips to the bakery were frequent and deliciously wonderful.

Then something happened. My daughter was diagnosed with two autoimmune diseases. As I began searching for ways to heal her little immune system one thing was recommended over and over again - a gluten-free diet. And so we turned to the dark side.

All of a sudden I was doing the one thing I thought I could NEVER do.
It was hard.
I'm not gonna lie. At first I felt some cravings so strong they led to an embarrassingly real grieving. I was devastated at not being able to slather cream cheese on that thick toasted piece of goodness. It was a major challenge to re-order our lives without some of the food that had been central to our diet. I had to learn new recipes and try different things.

But do you know what? I learned something really important in our shift to a gluten-free diet.

Bagels are not as important as I thought they were.

What's the one thing you think you could NEVER do?
The one thing that would be too hard to give up?
The one thing that you can't imagine making it through the week without?

What if you did?

Every year, just before Easter, many followers of Christ celebrate Ash Wednesday. For the redeemed ones, it is the day that marks the beginning of our slow, deliberate walk to the cross and the resurrection alongside our Savior.

We prepare to celebrate Easter not because chocolate bunnies are tasty or because it will be socially acceptable to wear white again in the South.

We prepare to celebrate because it is the day we remember our God did something many thought could NEVER be done. He conquered death to give us everlasting life.

If you have never practiced the spiritual discipline of fasting maybe this is a good time to give it a try. Whether it is the season of Lent or not, you can still enter into a place of sacrifice and submission.

Not because it is required of you.
Not because it is evidence that you are strong.
Not because it will earn you extra points with God.
Not because everybody's doing it.

Instead maybe, just maybe, your heart and mind will be transformed by the truth that the one thing you thought you could NEVER do is actually possible.

And maybe, just maybe, you will find that in your weakness the Spirit of God in you is made stronger.

And maybe, just maybe, you will watch as right before your very eyes that one thing becomes less important and the One who gave his very life that you might live becomes more important.

In light of His sacrifice, what might we sacrifice?

106

In hopes of drawing closer to Him, what might we walk farther away from?

Whatever you choose -
chocolate, TV, social media, Starbucks, shopping, your favorite coffee creamer that you just can't imagine life without.
Whatever it is...
It's not about that one thing and what you are doing or not doing about it.
It's about what God will do in its absence.

~ What is the one thing you could never do? Or never do without? What might happen if you did? In prayer, ask God to reveal these things and show you where he might desire abstinence in your life.

Some days I want to write, need to write. But I'm drowning in life. Ever feel that way? Maybe a meager few words are all we need to re-open lines of communication with our Savior. Here are some I have offered on my drowning days.

Give me a new heart, Lord.

This one is full of bitterness, impatience, anger, frustration, and restlessness.

Life feels like drudgery. I'm desperate for joy. I'm looking for it everywhere. You keep showing me glimpses but the darkness takes back over. It is so heavy, so suffocating.

I can't breathe.

The breath I do have I waste on screaming in anger or sobbing in frustration. I want my breath to be full of grace and gentleness, blowing life into my children, my husband, my family and friends. When your word says you give strength to the weary I want to feel it, not just read it.

I'm weary, drifting, homeless.

I can't keep up – always behind.

I'm frantic, without an anchor, being swept wherever the day's wild winds carry me. I know you can find a way to steady me here, in the middle of the chaos.

Steady me, Lord. Lighten my load.

For days on end the same scenario plays out – sunrise to sunset with no real breathing in between.

Days begin full of heavy burden, not hopeful expectation. They end full of restlessness, not peace.

Take my heart in your hands.

Open it up so the hard places spill out and the softness returns.

Give me a new heart, Lord.

For I will take you out of the nations; I will gather you from all the countries and bring you back into your own land. I will sprinkle clean water on you, and you will be clean; I will cleanse you from all your impurities and from your idols. I will give you a new heart and put a new spirit in you; I will remove from you your heart of stone and give you a heart of flesh. And I will put my spirit in you
{Ezekiel 36}

~ Consider the current condition of your heart. Where are the hard places? The ones filled with bitterness and frustration. Write a prayer confessing them to God and asking him to give you a new heart. Describe how that new heart would look and feel and manifest itself in your life.

Teach those who are rich in this world not to be proud
and not to trust in their money, which is so unreliable.
Their trust should be in God, who richly gives us all we need for our
enjoyment.
{1 Timothy 6:17}

I didn't really want this verse. Wouldn't be my first pick, if I was picking. I'm just saying. But some days God takes us where we don't want to go and it turns out he knew exactly what he was doing. Here's where those unwanted words led me.

If you are reading this, you are probably rich.
You have access to books and
you know how to read and
you actually have a little bit of free time to do that reading.

You likely have much more wealth and resources at your disposal than most of the world.

But our budget is tight, you may say.
I would nod my head and say *yes, I feel that way too.*

But those figures wouldn't feel so constricting if we sold a car or moved into a smaller house or bought less clothes or drank less coffee. You know what I mean.

So if we can agree we are all rich compared to the rest of the world, let's see what we can glean from this passage.

I notice there's no condemnation for being rich. Okay, that's nice. We aren't told we should feel bad about our position. Paul doesn't suggest we should take a guilt trip for having so much. The warning is in how we live with our wealth. That's the part that's so hard for me to stomach.

proud :: feeling a deep sense of pleasure over an act, possession, quality, or relationship by which one measures one's self-worth

Another translation says 'haughty' which suggests arrogance and a sense of superiority.

Yuck.

If we are considered rich, we are warned against one thing - being so proud and arrogant that we trust our wealth more than we trust our God.

That's not me. No way. Money is definitely not more important to me than God.

I believe it, but do I live it?

When I wake up in the morning do I rely on God to give me a word I need to start the day off right or do I rely on my money to buy me the perfect latte I *must* have to get going?

When I have some free time in my days am I more likely to seek out ways to serve God by serving others or do I think of ways I could use my money to pay someone else to serve me?

When the day has blown up in my face and the kids are crying and my patience is dwindling do I seek out the one who promises to single-handedly replace my anxieties with peace or do I depend on some diversion that my money can buy like TV or ice cream? Maybe both?!

With every decision of my day do I focus more on what my money can buy or on what Jesus has already bought?

Where am I really placing my trust and my hope?

Are the 'things' around me creating such a false sense of security and comfort that I am blind to my dependence on them? How can I live surrounded by worldly wealth and not let it distract me from the eternal riches that are being held out for me every single day?

This is the wrestling of the wealthy. We all must get in the ring and fight it to the death. When the power of money dies our life in Christ can truly begin.

~ In what specific ways do you sense God is calling you to shift your focus from the things that money can buy to the things only he can provide? What are the material things you would hate to have to do without? And what if you did?

I think God chuckles and shakes His head at me much of the time. He's probably even rolled His eyes a time or two.

I didn't set out to live a life planned by me instead of Him, it just happened by accident. Subconsciously, I did my best to build a nice, safe little Christian life. Somewhere along the way though, I got so busy planning everything and having five and ten year plans, that I became almost ineffective in my walk with the Lord.

It wasn't that I had never said 'yes' to the Lord, it was just that everything I gave him the thumbs up on was easy. Or at least easy-ish and straightforward and something that would fit into my pre-existing plans. My plans were my safety net and they were keeping me from hearing God's more significant promptings.

One day, while sitting on my favorite green wooden park bench in Seattle, the realization hit me: I was missing something. As I looked out over the ferry boats dreamily floating from downtown to the San Juan islands and the Space Needle pointing to the sky, I prayed. With my journal in my lap and Bible by my side, I prayed the Lord would use me - REALLY use me. I knew my plans were good. After all, they were meticulously laid out. The life I'd created for myself was out of the box without being too scary or going too far outside of my comfort zone.

That day, while looking out at the sparkle of the sun upon the waves, hearing the sound of seagulls, and the hubbub of a thriving city below, I knew there was more. I heard God's still small voice not because He had started talking, but because I had slowed down enough to listen. Closing my eyes, I realized this quote by J. A. Shedd was true,

A ship in harbor is safe, but that's not what ships are built for.

I knew safety was what I ultimately craved. I had no idea what leaving my safe harbor would mean. God continued to whisper the word "more" into my heart. My heart began to race as it occurred to me that I'd never consulted Him on anything I had planned for myself. As my mind continued to reel, it became abundantly clear that there wasn't much choice. Either I was going to go with Him, or I wasn't. I needed to quit trying to write God's story for my life and lean into the idea that He actually had His own written for me.

Exhaling slowly, I closed my eyes and opened my hands.

Send me

I whispered those words into the crisp Seattle air. To where? I had no idea. To do what? I was not yet told. But I knew it must begin with faith and trust. I liked the idea of trusting God and had placed my hope in Him since I was small, but this was different. This was intangible and big and weighty.

I didn't wake up the next morning knowing God was going to flip my life upside down in the best way possible, but little by little, Christ began shifting my priorities and allowing me to dream a little bigger. And then bigger than that. Somehow I became comfortable with being very uncomfortable. I no longer lived a life of safety, nor did I have life all figured out. In fact, as I began to embrace uncertainty and mystery and discomfort, my relationship with my Heavenly Father intensified and engulfed into an all-out fire. Lack of safety and joy somehow went hand-in-hand as I begun to say *Yes* to Him, giving God control of more than just the little things in my life.

Don't get me wrong, I was scared to death. I still am. But over and over, He has opened my eyes and heart to evidence in the Bible of other ordinary people who have also told Him *Yes* and *Send me*, to prove I'm not alone in my fear and reluctance. Even when things seem simply too big for little 'ole me.

Now when they saw the boldness of Peter and John, and perceived
that they were uneducated, common men, they were astonished.
And they recognized that they had been with Jesus.
{Acts 4:13}

Our Heavenly Father uses ordinary men and women who love Him. He uses regular people like you and me, regardless of our feelings of inadequacy and incapability. In fact, he uses us as a *result* of them. Because along with those feelings of inadequacy is a dependence on the Lord, knowing it is not in our own strength that we do things, but in *His* strength.

We know God is worthy of our trust and obedience so we don't have to ask – *Is it safe?* Just hop on the boat as He guides you out of the harbor. Thinking small won't change your life, and it certainly won't change the world. You were built for more.

~ What areas of your life are you 'playing it safe'?
~ Find a favorite spot and spend some just observing your surroundings. Write about what you see. Quiet your own agenda and listen for his. Write about what you hear.
~ If you weren't so concerned with safety, what nudging from God might you follow through on?

Today is your third 'Finders Keepers'.

{1} Open your Bible {or turn it on}.

{2} Find your verse. You can randomly choose. You can search for a keyword. You can flip to a particular chapter. You can go back to something you were recently intrigued by.
Or choose one from the list below:
~ Hebrews 10:35
~ 1 Corinthians 16:13
~ Romans 14:23
~ John 15:5
~ 2 Chronicles 20:12
Take a breath, allow yourself to be guided to that spot, and then see what you find. This isn't the time to go back to an old favorite. It's time to discover something new.

{3} Read your verse. Read it again. And again. Look at it in various translations. Read 2 or 3 verses surrounding it if you need some context. As you read, don't be too focused on how you can say something profound about the verse, but instead allow the verse to say something profound to you. Even if it's slow going at first, give it some time.

{4} 15 minutes flat. Set your timer. After you've taken a little time to let the words settle into your spirit take 15 minutes to record what you've found. If you have trouble coming up with anything, just copy the verse. Underline words or phrases that resonate with you. Write something about that word or phrase. Remember you are not being graded and there is no 'right' or 'wrong'. Stick to your time limit because if you feel the need to do more you may not do it at all, and that would be a shame.

DAY 21 *Dinner for Two* by Elizabeth Maxon

I had just finished scarfing down a bagel in my car when I read
it. Sometimes when the kids are not around I eat something that is
not gluten-free. Shhhh – don't tell my gluten-free family.

I thought to myself - give him an inch and he takes a mile.
I give him a mustard seed and he moves a mountain.
I offer a quiet breath of a prayer and he writes big bold truths on my
heart.
I sit in defiance and self-reliance and his love comes sweeping in to
rescue me.

It was just another crazy busy day. I know we all have them despite
the fact that I feed myself the lie
I am the CRAZIEST and BUSIEST person EVER.
{How's that for prideful?}

I had 15 minutes between finishing one appointment and the opening
of the library and the beginning of another. I was literally thinking
of what other errand or task I could squeeze into the 15 minutes so
that I would not waste one. single. moment.
Crazy.
Busy.
Get my drift?

On this particular day I fought off my achievement-oriented demons,
cruised through the drive-thru at Dunkin Donuts for a decaf and a
bagel.
I drove up the road, parked under a Bradford Pear tree in the empty
library parking lot,
And opened the sunroof {straight up one of my most favorite things
in the world - a minivan with a sunroof. I am so totally spoiled}. I
reclined the seat back so I could look up through the holes in the tree
to the blue sky. After wiping the cream cheese from my face, I took
a deep breath and relaxed.

With one finger tap on the little Bible App icon I invited Him into that space with me. It required very little effort really. But in an instant he reminded me of the importance of that moment, permanently carving a new truth on my heart.

Give Him an inch. He will take you miles.

I stand at the door and knock.
If anyone hears my voice and opens the door, I will come in to him
and eat with him, and he with me.
{Revelation 3:20}

I know what I need to survive but I don't always give it the time and attention it deserves. This is true of food for my body and food for my soul. The bagel was a poor choice, but the time in his word was a good one.

I imagined Jesus there outside my minivan door knocking. Or maybe he had climbed up on top and was tapping on the sunroof. I thought about me on the other side so busy checking off my to-do list, making calls, checking emails, and allowing my life to be so busy and loud that I may never have even heard it...
the
tap
tap
tap
of His hand.

And yet by His grace I got slow and quiet enough to notice and to open the window, open the door.
That was all I had to do.
Slow.
Quiet.
Open.

Give Him an inch. Just crack that door. And He enters in.

The living God steps into my presence and sits down over a meal with me. I don't even have to go to the trouble of preparing the meal or picking it up at the drive-thru. He comes with plates full of the finest food to satisfy me completely. Plates full of himself - the bread of life. {John 6:35}

And there is no scarfing down of that food. I savor every bite.

That's what sitting down to a meal is all about.

Slow.
Quiet.
Open.

Slow your busy hands.
Quiet your busy mind.
Open the door of your busy heart.

The maker of the stars wants to dine with you today.

~ Read the following verses and respond in your journal:
Matthew 17:20
Romans 8:26
1 John 4:19
~ Right now close your book, slow your breath, quiet your mind, and open the door of your heart. Give God just five minutes of silence and see what he has to say to you.

DAY 22 *Joy* by Elizabeth Maxon

Blindsided.

It means to be attacked when in a vulnerable position, to be hit by something you never even saw coming.

I was blindsided.

I stepped off of the elevator at the doctor's office full of hope and 10 minutes later, as I watched her 5-year-old finger press the 'down' button, I fought back tears.

I had been hit.

I was vulnerable.

I felt as if I were being attacked from all sides and I could barely stand.

I never saw it coming.

I played out the scenario in my head totally differently than it actually played out in real life.

The breathing got hard again.

I walked to the parking garage with each of their tiny hands in mine and the mask of a forced smile.

If I could just get them in the car and get my sunglasses on maybe I could release a bit of the floods welling up inside of me. I turned the radio up just loud enough that they couldn't hear my sobbing. I texted a friend because I needed somewhere for the kids to go so I could fall apart, all the way.

As I turned out of the parking deck I willed myself to breathe in deep and then it came back to me, the word that was whispered to me earlier on an ordinary Wednesday morning.

Joy

It didn't seem to fit on that catastrophic Thursday. And then it did. I remembered the context in which I had spoken it over that group of women I led.

120

The Lord has done great things for us and we are filled with joy.
{Psalm 126:3}

Because of what he has done.

Because he provided his son as a living sacrifice for me.

Because he wanted to bridge the gap between the darkness and heartache of this world to the beauty and light of eternity.

Because of what he has done, not because of what I want him to do right now or what he didn't do yesterday or what I'm hoping he will do tomorrow.

Because of what he has *done*

I don't just have joy,

I am <u>filled</u> with it.

It may be the most breathtakingly beautiful truth of my faith. In the hardest moments of this life, the deepest joy can be experienced.

Sometimes the words whispered on an ordinary Wednesday are the ones you will need on a catastrophic Thursday. Carry them close.

~ What great things has God done for you? Make a list. Go to him in worship and celebration, allowing him to lift your gaze from your fears and frustrations to his faithfulness.

~ Write down a verse or quote about 'joy' and add it to your collection of 'First-Last Thought' cards.

DAY 23 *Searching for the Sunrise* by Haley Barinowski

I have always been fascinated by sunrises.

Life forces later and later bedtimes, but the 'morning person' part of me still gets excited when I have to rise before the sun.

In the summer of 2013, I was privileged to spend a few weeks in Israel. One of our final stops was the Dead Sea. The night before we left for Jerusalem a group of us went out to the sea to watch the sunrise. The adventurous side of my heart was thrilled and couldn't care less that we only slept a few hours.

Despite all the anticipation, when the morning finally came - I wasn't impressed.

I wish I could say the view was straight off a postcard, trumpets were sounding majestically from the clouds, and the sun emerged over the pink mountains of Jordan in a fanfare of rich colors and bright light.

But it wasn't like that.

It was cloudy. The view was fuzzy. You couldn't quite see the sun itself.
I hesitate to say I was disappointed, but it certainly ended up being more about the experience of being in the Dead Sea at sunrise than about actually admiring the sunrise itself. We floated around in a haze of pinkish light, thoroughly enjoyed ourselves, and called it a success.

A year later I woke early to welcome another new day. This time my experience was much different.

I was in Washington D.C. and after an early morning airport drop-off I headed to the Lincoln Memorial to seek out the best view. I marched right up to the top of the marble stairs and parked myself directly in the center. I cherished the silence of that moment because there simply wasn't much you could say to describe what you saw.

Although other people joined me, the atmosphere was one of quiet awe, complete peace. There was a sense of unity and harmony as we all came together to appreciate this wondrous sight. Even in its silence, the experience eclipsed the noise of our busy-ness, our daily concerns, and our constant striving.

This time, there was no haze. The straight lines of the Washington Monument and the Reflecting Pool were clear. The dome of the Capitol was defined in the background. The colors of the sky were breathtaking. Life made sense. Everything was in perspective. The morning jolted from routine to sacred with just one look at the masterpiece in the sky.

As I sat in front of Abe for nearly an hour, my mind jumped to the gospel of Luke. These are the words of Zachariah, father of John the Baptist. He proclaims some important truths about the Savior. He begins by stating that his son John will be a prophet whose role is to···

···give to His people the knowledge of salvation
By the forgiveness of their sins,
Because of the tender mercy of our God,
*With which the **Sunrise** from on high will visit us,*
To shine upon those who sit in darkness and the shadow of death,
To guide our feet into the way of peace.
Luke 1:77-79

This verse inside of me and the view in front of me joined hands. I saw Jesus in a new way.

The Sunrise from on high.

What a remarkable way to describe our Savior. In that historical moment leading up to the removal of the barrier between humanity and divinity, I picture the Hallelujah Chorus playing a magnificent crescendo resulting in the incarnation of Christ.

After 400 years of silence and a millennia of darkness, God was about to erupt onto the scene of history in the most unbelievable sunrise, introduce the dawning of a new day, and *shine upon those who sit in darkness and the shadow of death.*

That would have been enough.

God could have entered time in a brilliant display of His glory, made some broad sweeping statements for all mankind, and left with a flourish. He could have just provided us with a few pointers about how to fix our messed-up lives and then promptly returned to his throne.

He didn't do that.

He went much further than that. He took a personal interest in *me*. He saw the darkness that controlled *my* heart and He graciously chose to shine into *my* life. And yours.

For God, who said,
'Light shall shine out of darkness,'
is the One who has shone in our hearts to give the Light of the
knowledge of the glory of God in the face of Christ.
2 Corinthians 4:6

He has shone *in our hearts.*

He has given me my own personal sunrise. My night of being controlled by sin is over, and a new day in my story has begun.

At first, I felt justified in being disappointed with the hazy Dead Sea sunrise. I thought I was entitled to have a moving, jaw-dropping experience, but instead I got a cloudy view with no real glimpse of the sun.

But that's faith, isn't it?

The Sunrise in my heart is certainly not always overflowing with clarity and confidence and sure answers. The lines aren't always clearly defined. Life isn't neatly compartmentalized.

I love the moments when I can feel the love of the Lord and hear Him clearly. But, if I'm honest, many times when I expect a brilliant sunrise in my time with the Lord, I can't even see the sun for the clouds.

I really want a Lincoln Memorial walk of faith, but most days I feel like I'm at the Dead Sea.

But here's the best part about the sun...

It still rises every morning. Even when it's not much more than a soft pink light, it is still there whether I can see it clearly or not. My inability to recognize God does not determine his presence or his power in my life. It is still there – every morning, every moment. That Dead Sea sunrise may not have appeared bold and bright to me, but it was still doing its job. It was still present. Still powerful.

It's really no wonder my faith often feels cloudy and fuzzy and frustrating. Relating to a divine Being isn't something that can be scripted. His attributes are far above my understanding, and His decisions are far outside of my time frame. Even *though* He knew I would be unfaithful and confused and doubtful, He still wanted to place a little piece of His sunrise in my heart so that I would walk around in the darkness carrying His light.

As I get to know the ultimate Sunrise more and more, my prayer is that my little sunrise will look more and more like Him.

So whether it is at the lowest place on earth, in front of a national monument, in the pages of Scripture, or the daily moments of grace - *may we keep searching for the sunrise.*

~ Consider finding a time this week to go and watch the sunrise. You'll be glad you did!

~ What is one area of your relationship with God where His working seems hazy or unclear?

~ What are three ways He has shown His faithfulness in that area despite the clouds?

~ To keep digging, read Luke 1:68-79 and/or 2 Corinthians 4:3-11.

DAY 24 *This is Only a Test* by Elizabeth Maxon

There is this crazy story about Jesus feeding five thousand people with five loaves and two fish.

For those of us who believe the Bible as truth, this is one of the miracles of Jesus. An impossible act is made possible. But there is something else about this passage. There is something significant on the other side of the feeding of the 5000. The side where the disciples were just hanging out with Jesus and found themselves face-to-face with a multitude of hungry people. Pre-miracle is a very different perspective than post-miracle.

Before the feeding of the 5000 Jesus asks Philip, one of his disciples, *'Where are we to buy bread, so that these people may eat?'*, which as it turns out was not a question Jesus actually needed the answer to. He already had the answer. The scriptures tell us *'He said this to test him, for he himself {Jesus} knew what <u>he</u> {Jesus} would do.'*

Have you ever wondered if God tests you? I think he does, but maybe not in the way you think.

He doesn't test you like a strict Catholic nun teacher tests you with a stick in hand ready to strike if you get the answer wrong.
He doesn't test you like a bitter jealous girlfriend who tries to set you up with a question like - *'Tell me the truth or I will break up with you! Did you look at that girl when she walked by!?!'*
He doesn't test you with a 'pass' or 'fail' on the line.
He tests you like we 'test' the water before we jump in
or 'test' a line before we cast it into the lake.

God 'tests' to get a better idea of the conditions. Not the conditions of the water or the line, but of our hearts. The result of those tests are really meant for us. They are meant to let us know how much or little we are seeing the world around us from His perspective.

I think God's test for you may look something like it might have looked for Philip.

He invites us into a problem or a situation that seems impossible. Perhaps he asks us a question to which we would likely respond, *'I can't. That's impossible.'*

Where do we buy the bread for 5000 people out here in the middle of nowhere with no money?

Umm...we don't, Jesus. That's impossible.

And we respond either like Philip {stating the impossibility of the situation} -

Two hundred denarii worth of bread would not be enough for each of them to get a little.

Or like Andrew {perhaps skeptical but at least giving Jesus something to work with}-

There is a boy here who has five barley loaves and two fish, but what are they for so many?

And then Jesus – oh, how I love him. He doesn't pull out a red marker and draw a big 'F' on anybody's face. He doesn't dish out reprimands or shake his head in disgust over the lack of faith.

No. Jesus just does it. He does what he knew he was going to do all along.
He makes the impossible possible.

But wait. He didn't just do it. He let the disciples be a part of it! Under his direction they were actually the ones to do the feeding. Jesus performed the miracle in their hands and they offered the miracle to the multitude. It wasn't the first or last time we see it happen in the Bible. Read for yourself and you'll find that making the impossible possible was actually Jesus' M.O. And time and time again he invited ordinary people like me and you to be a part of it. He still does it today.

What part of your life right now are you shaking your head and saying...

Umm...Jesus, that's impossible. I can't.

Spend some time thinking about it because I'd be willing to bet that is the very place that he already has a plan to show you that He can.

And, by the way, don't beat yourself up if you feel like your faith and your perspective is too limited to see how God could possibly do 'that thing'. You are pre-miracle right now. If you follow his direction, things will look completely different on the other side.

~ What seems impossible in your life right now? What simple thing do you hold in your hands that you could offer to Jesus and allow him to do something miraculous with?
~ Read John 6:1-14 and respond in your journal.

DAY 25 *Loved* by Elizabeth Maxon

Maybe you've struggled with really accepting God's complete love and devotion to you. Maybe you are fairly certain he is an adoring Father, but you could still use some affirmation.

If so, today is the day to be reminded of this truth.

Set your timer for 15 minutes. Read the Message translation of this passage from Ephesians 1. I have replaced all the references to 'us' with 'me' so that we can fully grasp how personal it is. Once you are finished reading, sit silently with your eyes closed in his embrace until your timer goes off.

Long before he laid down earth's foundations, he had me in mind, had settled on me as the focus of his love, to be made whole and holy by his love. Long, long ago he decided to adopt me into his family through Jesus Christ. (What pleasure he took in planning this!) He wanted me to enter into the celebration of his lavish gift-giving by the hand of his beloved Son. Long before I first heard of Christ and got my hopes up, he had his eye on me, had designs on me for glorious living.

~ You're already so adored. Listen to the song 'He Knows My Name' by Francesca Battistelli and be reminded.
~ Pull out your journal and complete this sentence.
When God looks at me he sees...

There is a thread weaving its way through all of my readings lately. What I think God is trying to tell me is this:

You have no idea what you're doing.
Your thoughts are all messed up.
You have no control over anything.

Thanks, God. I get it. You're God and I'm not.

Our culture, of which I am a product, is obsessed with self-help.

How to get skinnier,
have a better marriage,
succeed at work,
get along with your kids,
make better friendships,
keep your current friendships...
The list goes on and on.

The magazine titles and self-help sections in the book store will confirm this. We want all the steps to all the things to improve all our lives.

In the meantime, I've seen only one thing have a long-lasting impact in my life: the power of Jesus's healing of my mind, body and soul to bring about change.

I am a better mother, sister, daughter, worker, servant, and person when Jesus comes in and changes me from the inside out. My heart changes first. Soon my words, actions, habits and outlook follow.

I know. That's a Sunday School answer. But it doesn't mean it's easy. It means we really can't step our way into any change. We simply have to believe the answer is found ultimately in him. And if that is true, we need to find ourselves in him if we're going to find the answers.

It all sounds sort of mystical. And really, I think it is. I have experienced more healing and life change lying on my daughter's bed crying in prayers of surrender for 20 minutes than I ever have on any self-help plan.

I have come to believe the only real self-help plan is to help myself to Jesus. I don't mean in the same way of helping myself to another plate at dinner.
I mean helping myself get to those moments with him. For this, I need to ask myself two questions.

1. What is keeping me from Jesus?
Is it too much TV, too many commitments, or too little focus? For a while I was spending hours every night on the couch in front of a screen. Maybe for you it's something else. Yes, we have to live life. We can't be on our knees in prayer 100% of the time, but grocery shopping, diaper changing, coffee making, and even TV watching can center around him. If our center is Him. But, sometimes our DVRs are too full and we've stretched ourselves too thin and our schedules are too crammed to find a moment to get to Jesus. So, find your distractions. Minimize them. If necessary, get rid of them completely.

2. How do I experience Jesus?
It's fine to rid yourself of distractions, but if you only replace it with other distractions you're not helping yourself to Jesus at all. We have to find out how we experience Jesus best. Do you hike? Do you paint? Do you serve? Do you sing? Do you write? What are the moments in which you experience him?
Find those and do those more in place of your distractions. Because I experience Jesus when I am reading and writing I choose that over TV as often as possible.

When I do these things Jesus teaches me <u>all</u> the things I need to know to be a better wife, a better worker, a better parent, and a better friend.

When I find time to listen he whispers to me –
You don't have a parent-sized hole in your soul.
Or a husband-sized hole.
Or a man-sized hole.
Or a child-sized hole.
You have a God-sized hole.

If you are feeling empty, tired, unfulfilled, lost, or joyless, may I suggest you stop trying to hastily fill your soul with anything and everyone and finally slow down enough to feed your soul what it is meant to be fed—God and God alone.

The best self-help is helping myself to Jesus.

> *There is a God-shaped vacuum in the heart of every person,*
> *and it can never be filled by any created thing.*
> *It can only be filled by God,*
> *made known through Jesus Christ.*
> – Blaise Pascal

If you want to dig into a big delicious meal, you'll need a fork and a knife.

I love to cook. Really, I do. But with the pace of life these days, I have to admit, I absolutely savor a meal prepared *for* me. It doesn't happen often, so when it does I allow the sight, smell and taste of it to really sink in. My heart {and taste buds} give thanks.

I've been thinking a lot about things prepared for me.

I've also been reading a lot about Abraham.

I'm guessing most of you are familiar with the name. It's amazing really, considering he should have just drifted off into obscurity. Before God got a hold of him some people may have labeled Abraham a 'nobody'. He had no children, no storybook marriage, no impressive achievements. And yet I can say with great confidence that he is the 'father of my faith'.

Andy Stanley says this of the story of Abraham -
Despite our relentless disinterest in him, God made the first move to reestablish his connection with humankind.

Adam and Eve majorly messed up our original divine relationship with that well-known fruit eating incident. In that moment we saw *the massive, forever-changing impact a lack of faith in God can bring.*

Enter Abraham.

In that man we see *the massive, forever-changing impact that a bit of faith in God can bring.*

and Abram believed the Lord,
and the Lord counted him as righteous because of his faith.
{Genesis 15:6}

It all started with a promise. God made a promise to do something seemingly impossible in the life of an ordinary man.

It all moved forward with a response. The course of history was changed by Abraham responding in faith. An ordinary man, trusting an extraordinary God, to ultimately serve up the life he had prepared in advance for him - the very life and purpose that Abraham had been created for.

Do you ever hear whispers of a life prepared for you? Do you ever sense an uncovering of something so deep in your soul that it almost feels like it was knit into your very being?

When the Creator enters into relationship with His creation there is an unspeakable feeling of being understood for who you really are and for who you were really meant to be. If you don't know what I am talking about keep digging. Keep listening. I promise it's there, waiting like a glowing ember just under the surface of your skin.

I'm learning that I sometimes must battle my intense work ethic and sense of responsibility. There comes a time when I must cease working my tail off for whatever it is I think I *should* be doing. Instead I must believe in what has already been prepared for me.

Sometimes I take off my apron, dust the flour from my cheeks, and just sit down at the table. I purposefully take hold of the fork and knife and dive into what has been plated and served just for me.

Sometimes I must stop giving myself rigid requirements or restrictions. I step away from the burden of preparing a perfect meal. Instead I accept that which I have been served. And I savor every bite.

This proverbial meal is not nearly as easy to consume as the bowl of chili I had for dinner last night. In order to really partake of the life uniquely prepared just for me, I have to overcome the countless distractions that beckon me away from the table. It's the distractions we will have to target. We will have to make a conscious effort to let go of idle time spent in fruitless endeavors. And with the extra time we bank we can do glorious things like - reading, writing, memorizing scripture, creating works of art, having real conversations, and looking people in the eyes.

What about you? What do you want more of? What are the things that will allow you to savor every bite - whether bitter or sweet - of this life prepared just for you? What are the things that will leave you and those around you feeling satisfied instead of suffering from hunger pangs?

I'm asking myself all these same questions over and over again because I will never allow my soul to be given over to a 'relentless disinterest' in the One who created me in this time and this place for the work He prepared just for me.

Now God has us where he wants us, with all the time in this world and the next to shower grace and kindness upon us in Christ Jesus. Saving is all his idea, and all his work. All we do is trust him enough to let him do it. It's God's gift from start to finish! We don't play the major role. If we did, we'd probably go around bragging that we'd done the whole thing! No, we neither make nor save ourselves. God does both the making and saving. He creates each of us by Christ Jesus to join him in the work he does, the good work he has gotten ready for us to do, work we had better be doing.
{Ephesians 2:7-10}

~ Respond to this reading and the passage from Ephesians in your journal. Write down key words or phrases that jumped out at you. Make note of anything specific God brought to mind in your own life.

Here's a fun fact for you.

It takes me half as much time as it takes my husband to mow the grass.

I'm not bragging. I'm just stating a fact.

But there was a time when I secretly thought I was better than other people because I could get things done faster. I could accomplish more in one day than some people could in one month.

This one difference between me and my husband {among a vast number of similarities} once threatened the health of my marriage. It still can on occasion if I'm not careful.

When you live at an accelerated pace {which means your body and mind operate in turbo mode}, there is a tendency to get frustrated with those who are, well, slower.

For most of my life
slow = bad.
slow = lazy.
slow = lack of interest.
slow = going nowhere.

And then I met my husband.

I didn't find him to be bad, lazy, lacking interest, or headed nowhere. I did find him to move at a snail's pace compared to me.

At first this was very attractive. It felt good for my racing legs to rest and wait for him to catch up. Later I grew frustrated.

When I wanted to paint the entire house in one weekend and he wanted to take breaks to watch deer in the backyard {it's not like they're endangered species or anything, are they??}.

When I wanted to drive straight through to our destination and he

137

wanted to stop and go inside a restaurant to actually sit down and eat {seriously...isn't that what drive-thrus are for?!}.

When I wanted to go ahead and get everything hung up on the walls in our new house and he had to hunt down a stud finder and level to make sure they were perfect {what ever happened to 'eyeballing' it?!}. When I scheduled something for us to do two nights in a row and he told me he needed more 'down time' at home {what the heck is 'down time'??}.

Here's the thing about a sprinter marrying a stroller - you learn you're actually good for each other. Because I love Joey and see so much good in him I've seen the beauty in slowing down. On the flip side, I think he would agree that trying to keep up with me at times has been, well, maybe almost exhilarating {and sometimes exhausting}.

One afternoon Joey was mowing the lawn and I sat down on the back porch and watched him. The kids were playing in the yard and there was a breeze blowing through the screen. I propped my feet up on the table and allowed myself to stare off through the trees.

At one point Lucy ran up onto the porch and looked at me like I had two heads - *Why are you looking like that mommy?* The poor child rarely sees me without my eyes locked and loaded on something.

A moment later I heard the lawnmower cut off. Joey had stopped a third of the way into his cutting to look at the crabapple tree in the middle of our yard. At first I laughed to myself because the behavior was so predictable. But then, I watched with admiration and joy as he touched the leaves and walked around the perimeter of full foliage. I saw him reach up into one of the branches and pull off one of the apples. He put it up to his mouth. I could see him really tasting it, not rushing his bites. He stood there for a few minutes eating and looking around the yard. Then the lawn mower started back up.

I considered the fact that I never would have done that. When I turn the mower on, it runs straight through until I am finished. My eyes never leave the uncut grass in front of me.

It couldn't have been more than 10 minutes later that I heard the hum of the mower slow to a stop again. This time he was looking up at me. He took his earbuds out and asked,
Hey - have you ever actually eaten one of those crabapples?
I couldn't remember.
They're pretty good.

Again he stepped away from the mower. This time he walked across the yard and began searching the tree for the perfect one. The kids ran it up to me and I took a bite.
It was good.

Do you remember the story of God creating the heavens and the earth?
Do you remember how throughout this monumental process he would stop work and consider all he had accomplished and then declare it 'good'?

If it were not for my unhurried husband I wonder how many times I would actually pause my work to declare it 'good'. How many moments in this life has he slowed me down long enough to actually enjoy instead of passing by on my race to the next thing?

Beauty is found in the slowing.
It's why I write.
It's why I take pictures.
It's why I go on walks through gardens.
It's why I'm simplifying my life.
It's why I married my husband.

~ What slows you down? And when you do, what do you find to declare 'good'?

~ Write down a quote or a passage of scripture that helps you remember to slow down and savor. Add it to your 'First-Last Thought' collection.

~ Now do it – slooooooow down. Sit still and find something beautiful to gaze at with your eyes, or something delicious to savor in your mouth, or something smooth and soft to hold in your hands.

Today is your fourth 'Finders Keepers'.

{1} Open your Bible {or turn it on}.

{2} Find your verse. You can randomly choose. You can search for a keyword. You can flip to a particular chapter. You can go back to something you were recently intrigued by.

Or choose one from the list below:

~ Hebrews 10:35

~ 1 Corinthians 16:13

~ Romans 14:23

~ John 15:5

~ 2 Chronicles 20:12

Take a breath, allow yourself to be guided to that spot, and then see what you find. This isn't the time to go back to an old favorite. It's time to discover something new.

{3} Read your verse. Read it again. And again. Look at it in various translations. Read 2 or 3 verses surrounding it if you need some context. As you read, don't be too focused on how you can say something profound about the verse, but instead allow the verse to say something profound to you. Even if it's slow going at first, give it some time.

{4} 15 minutes flat. Set your timer. After you've taken a little time to let the words settle into your spirit take 15 minutes to record what you've found. If you have trouble coming up with anything, just copy the verse. Underline words or phrases that resonate with you. Write something about that word or phrase. Remember you are not being graded and there is no 'right' or 'wrong'. Stick to your time limit because if you feel the need to do more you may not do it at all, and that would be a shame.

Have you ever noticed how many people don't pay attention to the flight attendant giving the pre-takeoff speech?

You know the one - pointing to the exits, demonstrating the seat belts, and instructing everyone on the use of oxygen masks. Next time you fly, look around. Our heads are buried in books or devices. Our earbuds signal we're not to be bothered. We don't want to be···interrupted.

But what happens when life as usual gets interrupted, when turbulence occurs? Will you remember to put your oxygen mask on first before helping your children? Do you know which exit is closest in case you need to find it? Will you wish you had paid attention to how to use the seat as a flotation device?

It's easy to praise God in the good times. We say we're #blessed. But following Jesus doesn't mean we're guaranteed an easy, breezy existence. Actually we're guaranteed quite the opposite. We are going to face hard times.

In my own life, losing people I love has brought great pain because loving them had brought great joy. Isn't that a difficult but beautiful truth? Within a few recent years of each other, both of my parents died. In the wake of their deaths I have depended on and clung to my faith. My strength comes completely *from* Him, made possible only by my relationship *with* Him.

Knowing *about* God and having a relationship *with* Him are two different things.

How do we get close to someone? We spend time together. We learn about them. We spend time reading about the things they have said or done. The same is true for God. When we spend time with Him, read His word and talk to Him in prayer we grow closer to Him. By knowing what he *has* done we can be confident of what he *will* do.

How are we to know He can take all the hurt we've experienced and use it for good if we haven't read about the Israelites using the plunder after escaping Egypt?

How are we to trust that sometimes His ways don't make sense but always come together for the good of His children if we don't know about Zechariah and Elizabeth?

How are we to encourage one another to spend time with Him instead of running ourselves ragged making everything look great on the outside if we don't know about Mary and Martha and Jesus' big call out?

How are we to draw strength from Him when imprisoned in our own chains if we haven't read the letters of a shackled Paul?

How are we to leave our childhood homes and build new ones, sometimes far away from everything we've ever known, if we don't know about Ruth?

How do we face our own giants if we don't know about David and Goliath?

How do we listen for His still, small voice instead of looking for great big signs if we haven't read about Elijah?

How do we confidently cry out *Thy Will be Done* if we don't know of Jesus sweating drops of blood in the garden crying out the same thing?

Spending time in His word is an <u>invitation</u>. Let's allow our lives to be interrupted for that.

Let's interrupt our morning routine to begin each day seeking God.

Let's interrupt our to-do list to read our bible, asking God to reveal to us what He wants us to learn that day.

Let's interrupt our DIY attitude to learn something new from our greatest teacher.

Let's interrupt our 'hurry up and get there' lives to slow down and take time to draw close to the one who is waiting to give us directions.

If we accept the invitation to a life with Christ, we will arrive at our destination to find we have been used all along the way – through the smooth and rough parts of the journey.

Let us hold tightly without wavering to the hope we affirm,
for God can be trusted to keep his promise.
Hebrews 10:23

~ Write down one area of life you've got a super tight grip on. Pray over this area with God and admit that He's God, and you're not. Pray for him to take all your worry away in this situation. Thank Him for his provision in all of your life, this situation included. Ask for your intentions to line up with His purpose for you.

~ To go deeper explore Ephesians 3:14 - 20 in the NLT translation.

Have you ever had that awful feeling way down deep?

I call it a 'pit in my stomach' but it's really more like a wild, reckless tornado twisting and destroying any semblance of safety or peacefulness. It rearranges every thought and emotion that once seemed strong until they are left like broken pieces in a pile on the ground of my soul.

I am left with a choice - fight or flight?

Life gives us 'pit in your stomach' moments. It's what Jesus meant when he said - *in this world you will have trouble...*

We could stop right there and lose all hope but Jesus doesn't. He doesn't stop there.

...but take heart, I have overcome the world.

OK, well, that makes me feel a little bit better.

But Jesus doesn't stop there either.

What follows in chapter 17 of the book of John is what is sometimes referred to as the 'Prayer of the High Priest'. And it was spoken for me and you.

Jesus' request on my behalf has brought rivers of tears. Let it wash over you too.

I do not ask that you take them out of the world, but that you keep them from the evil one. They are not of the world, just as I am not of the world. Sanctify them in the truth; your word is truth. As you sent me into the world, so I have sent them into the world.

Sanctified.
Set apart.

A blessing prayed over my life - over your life - by Jesus himself.

This life I have chosen, this life of following Jesus - it isn't always easy.

And this world - oh this world - it will sweep you up into its distorted truths. It will pull you into the false promise of an 'easy' life if you just 'go with the flow'. And if you're not prepared to step heavy and hard directly into the current of this culture you will be taken down.

As a follower of Jesus I choose for my life and the lives of my children to be set apart. Every day I have to claim it anew. Some days the walk upstream is easy and refreshing. Other days the waters come rushing at me and I push against them with all my might - fighting to keep my head up.

When I find myself gasping for air I grab onto the only thing that can fill me back up with breath again - the truth.

Your word is truth.

With the waves crashing all around us and the current grabbing at our heels, how do we not get sucked in and swept away?

The answer is simple...
truth.

Sometimes truth acts as an anchor that keeps us from being carried away. Other times it's like a mask, an oxygen tank to keep us alive as we are thrust down into the deep dark parts of the ocean. And, every once in a while, it raises us up to take floating steps right across the crashing surf.

146

If you follow Jesus long enough - you eventually walk on water.

And so here we are - in this world, walking alongside darkness and brokenness, but carrying inside of us something whole and full of light. The evil one keeps trying to lock our hands together with all the sin we brush up against. We feel it - the oppression that is just waiting to grab onto us with both hands and pull us down into the rushing waters.

On days like these I am tempted to flee this world.
To flee the problems with no apparent solutions.
To flee the people I don't know how to 'fix'.

And then I return to the truth - the thing that sets me apart and sets me free.

Today in the truth of that prayer recorded by Jesus' beloved disciple I don't find the word 'flee' one single time.
Instead I find Jesus speaking one word over me like a gentle nudge.

Sent.

In those 26 short verses, he repeats it seven times.

> As you have sent me into the world,
> so I have sent them into the world.

And so I go, as I am sent.
I do not flee.

And why? Because I have been sent with a purpose.

> so that the world may believe...
> so that the world may know that you sent me and loved them even
> as you loved me.
> {John 17:23}

Today when faced with the choice - fight or flight? I fight.

But I don't step into the battle unarmed. The truth is my protection.
And I do it not for myself, but for the world - to whom I have been
sent.

~ Read John 17. Write down anything significant to you. In
particular, to whom and for what are you being sent? What
situations have you considered fleeing from where God would have
you fight?

Do you feel powerful?

She asked the question thoughtfully, helping me think through a challenging situation.

Um...

I paused. The question caught me off guard. Powerful? Well, no, actually. My situation involved another person and I can't control another person. So, powerful? No. I felt quite powerless, actually.

Then I felt a familiar nudge from God in my heart. I thought, *just because I don't have all the power — does that really make me powerless? A victim of another person's power? A victim of circumstance?*

No.

Just because I don't have all the power doesn't mean I don't have any power.

Just because I don't have all the control doesn't mean I don't have any control.

I do not have ALL the power or ALL the control. I do have some power. I do have some control. Learning to recognize what power and control I do have, and being responsible with it, can change everything.

Like a sailor who rightly acknowledges she cannot control the wind and the waves, do I surrender the boat and declare myself a victim of the sea? No. I put my oars in the water and row. I acknowledge what is in my control and take hold of it.

If it is possible, as far as it depends on you,
live at peace with everyone.
Romans 12:18

How far does it depend on me? What is within my power? What is within my control? What is not?

Ask God to help you surrender what is out of your control and take hold of what is within.

In Matthew 11:28 Jesus said,
Come to me, all you who are weary and burdened,
and I will give you rest.

What is in your power?
What is not?

If any of you lacks wisdom, you should ask God, who gives
generously to all without finding fault, and it will be given to you.
James 1:5

What is in your power?
What is not?

[Jesus said,] Here I am! I stand at the door and knock.
If anyone hears my voice and opens the door,
I will come in and eat with that person, and they with me.
Revelation 3:20

~ Journal about these two simple questions: What is in your power?
What is not?
~ Explore passages about the power of God. Choose one to add to your 'First-Last Thought' collection.

DAY 33 *Eyes on You* by Elizabeth Maxon

There are times when I wear out my fingers from typing and my knees from praying...
 all in search of answers.

Have you ever set out for answers and found yourself at the end of the road just holding more questions and confusion?

If thyroid disorders are an entire other world {and they are} I know about as much as the island of Bora Bora. There are vast oceans and land masses of information surrounding me that look completely foreign and overwhelming.

My daughter has a thyroid disorder so I want answers. Sometimes I get them and sometimes I don't. More than once the waters of uncertainty have risen up and over my shoulders, my mouth, my eyes, threatening to keep me from another deep breath. If you know what I mean, maybe these words will pull you back above the surface and save you too.

Jehoshaphat was King of Israel {that's God's people...the 'good guys'...but they were also sometimes bad...I digress...}. Jehoshaphat found out that a whole bunch of dudes were coming to attack his people - God's people. Not good.
Seemed overwhelming.
Seemed like the odds were not in their favor.
Seemed like victory was impossible.

So what did the king do?
He got scared.
Yeah. I would have too.
But that's not all.
He got scared, but he shifted his gaze from the situation invoking that fear to the One who could remove it.

Then Jehoshaphat was afraid and set his face to seek the Lord.
2 Chronicles 20:3

It appears as though the fear and the seeking of the Lord all happened in one fell swoop. There were no hours, days, weeks of agony before he finally decided maybe he should think about turning his face. {Note to self: Do this. Don't let the fear linger.}

The rest of 2 Chronicles 20 details the prayer of Jehoshaphat and the events that followed. I've read the events many times before. They have saved me from other drowning times. They end with God's people walking away victorious simply by
being still
letting God fight for them
lifting praises instead of swords
...all precious things God wants us to apply to our own lives. But there was one verse before all of that I had never really noticed before.

In his prayer, Jehoshaphat proclaims his powerlessness {source of fear} but also proclaims God's powerFULLness {source of hope}. Following that he makes this one simple statement that engraved itself deep into my heart...

We do not know what to do, but our eyes are on you.

I don't know what all her blood test results mean.
I don't know if we should talk to other doctors.
I don't know what is causing her to be an emotional wreck on a given day.
I don't know how to handle the fits of rage and tears full of sorrow.
I don't know if she will wake up tomorrow feeling good or feeling like her hormones are doing battle inside of her.

It feels so good to admit that sometimes - I. don't. know.

I don't know what to do...
but my eyes are on You.

When I put my problems in the periphery and God right in front of
me I move
from fear to hope
from drowning to breathing
from facing defeat to claiming the victory that is already mine.

If you're like me and you've been spending too much time focused on
what you don't know maybe you need this reminder to daily focus on
what you do know. God is a whole heck of a lot bigger and more
powerful than an army raised up against you.

~ If there is something invoking fear and anxiety right now, write it
down. Write down all the things you don't know, but wish you did.
Now turn to a fresh sheet of paper and remember all the things you
do know. Meditate on that one phrase – *We don't know what to
do but our eyes are on you.*

The wonder of it all is that You came
You came of Your own free will
You came leaving the glory of the heavenlies
You came for us, the joy set before You

The wonder of it all is that You came
You came wrapped as a helpless babe
You came embodied in human flesh
You came as fully God and fully man

The wonder of it all is that You came
You came to show us the Father's heart
You came and were acquainted with our sorrows
You came to simply dwell among us

The wonder of it all is that You came
You came to bring us life
You came to forgive our sins
You came to set captives free

You came then
And You come now
We needed you, but You wanted us
So, the wonder of it all turns out to be You

~ Write your own prayer or poem to worship and celebrate who
God – Father, Son, and Holy Spirit - has been to you.

By the end of the introduction, tears sat full and salty in my eyes.

Come outside now, it's getting dark. *

I had waited my whole life for that invitation.

I immediately loved Barbara Brown Taylor for offering it to me with a kind confidence - an invitation not to escape the darkness, but to willingly step into it.

Over the past few years I have ventured into places others may have warned against, but her words welcome me through their foreboding thresholds. She confirmed what I had long suspected, that there is an offering in even the most offensive of places. There are treasures only found in the shadows. There is a world full of wonders we anxiously lock away and I am ready to swing wide the gates.

I spent the evening talking with a group of college girls about fear. Some held theirs knowingly in their hands, others had to dig around to unearth the surface of them, and still others kept them locked away in the cellar of their souls. I could relate to each one.

The week before I had engaged my mother in the same conversation. She walked terrified through childhood afraid of things like being washed down the drain of the kitchen sink. As she grew into an adult her fears grew too, leading her to believe that maybe death would be the only road to a peace that life could not offer. She bravely resurrected her past demons in an attempt to help me address similar struggles in my own daughter. Recently I have seen simple worries give way to debilitating anxiety in her 7-year-old world. As I considered the fears of both my mother and my daughter I was reminded - I carry my own. Though the source is different, the course is nearly always the same.

*Brown Taylor, Barbara. *Learning to Walk in the Dark*. HarperOne, 2015.

Some of you know what I mean.

What is the source of your fear? What thing {or things} would you rather not discuss because it either pokes a hole for worry to drip through or slices right through the dam holding back the vast waters of anxiety?

I began to wonder as I sat on the porch swing, gently rocking myself awake, *what if we reached out and grabbed the hand of whatever is looming in the darkness?*

What if we were brave enough to touch that gray, wrinkled witch hand with the jagged yellow fingernails wriggling in our direction?

What if instead of shoving her behind a locked door, I felt my way up her arms, along her slender shoulders, onto her warm neck and allowed my fingers to explore the soft lines of her face?

Might I find something unexpected? Might her mouth be turned ever so slightly up in a smile that says, "Ah yes, you've finally found me." Might there be untold beauty and truth and grace and even peace on the other side of those witch hands, on the other side of the source of our fear?

I looked out from the porch and up into the cloud-covered sky. Not dark enough to turn on a light and not bright enough to wear sunglasses. Cloudy days are the perfect conditions for considering what might happen if we became equally comfortable in the darkness and the light. What might our blind eyes begin to see? What freedom might we find on the other side of fear?

~ Begin by practicing silence and solitude for five minutes. Set a timer. Close your eyes and breathe deep. Listen. {It may seem longer than you expect.}

~ Have you struggled with fear? What are the things you keep shoving back into the closet? Write them down in your journal and lay them before God. Allow him to shine light into the dark places and dispel your fears. Allow him to replace them with his peace, protection, and hope. What is the offering on the other side?

~ Look up 'fear' in the index of your Bible or search 'Bible passages about fear' on your computer. Write down the ones that speak most deeply to you. Carry them around in your pocket or post them on your bathroom mirror. Refer to them as often as needed and add them to your 'First-Last Thought' collection.

If you grew up in the 80's like me you probably remember She-Ra, Princess of Power. She was to little girls what He-Man and the Masters of the Universe were to little boys.

God brought Shera to mind recently.

I was sitting quietly for the first time in a long time. Baby girl was napping and the dog was snuggled at my side. It was magical. If you're a mama you know what I mean. It was raining outside and I could feel God's presence wrapping me up, encouraging me, and refreshing my soul. It's amazing how a little bit of stillness can do that. It can transform you. I needed to be transformed.

As I sipped my coffee, I felt God speak so clearly to me from the book of Ephesians. I had been feeling bare and vulnerable to arrows for weeks. The arrows kept coming faster than I could hold up my shield and block them. On that morning right in the middle of Ephesians 6 I pictured She-Ra. I pictured her with all her gear on, standing in strength and beauty. I had this image of her holding up her sword and shield dispelling every arrow thrown at her. It was a vivid mental picture of something I loved as a kid. But it was also something practical I could hold onto as an adult. There is a strength and beauty we can possess daily, no matter our feelings.

Maybe you've heard about the armor of God before. It's important because as followers of Christ we are faced with spiritual battles on a daily basis. I've found that just when God is trying to mold and shape us, to change us and allow us to move forward, the evil one delights in attacking us relentlessly.

The arrows look different but the hurt is the same. Some are the arrows of inadequacy. Others are the arrows of fear, depression and anxiety. Still others come flying at our self-image or our dreams. The list could go on and on. We all have things the evil one loves to painfully remind of us. They are meant to hurt us, derail us, take our eyes off our strength and song, our healer, our redeemer, our savior. But we are strength and beauty.

If we hold up our shield and block the arrows that are thrown, He gives us the power. We become a princess of power. I know this because He promises it in His word.

Finally, be strong in the Lord and in his mighty power. Put on the full armor of God, so that you can take your stand against the devil's schemes. For our struggle is not against flesh and blood, but against the rulers, against the authorities, against the powers of this dark world and against the spiritual forces of evil in the heavenly realms. Therefore, put on the full armor of God, so that when the day of evil comes, you may be able to stand your ground, and after you have done everything, to stand. Stand firm then, with the belt of truth buckled around your waist, with the breastplate of righteousness in place, and with your feet fitted with the readiness that comes from the gospel of peace. In addition to all this, take up the shield of faith, with which you can extinguish all the flaming arrows of the evil one. Take the helmet of salvation and the sword of the Spirit, which is the word of God.
Ephesians 6:10-17

What if we were all intentional about suiting up and seeking truth? What if we allowed him to fill us and cover us with his righteousness? What if we stood sure-footed in peace? What if we boldly held out our faith in the face of flying arrows? What if we let salvation fall on our heads and the Spirit do the fighting for us?

I want to be His princess of power. I want my strength and beauty to be the result of the changes he is making in me.

~ If you haven't done it already, try out the 4 P's today – pour, passage, process, pray. Use this reading and the included passage from Ephesians as your starting point.

I don't like waiting.
I like movement.
I don't like stopping.
I like starting.

And so I sit {uncomfortably} still and let these words knead and shape my heart, making it into something different.

Cease striving and know that I am God... {Psalm 46:10}

Those who wait for the Lord will gain new strength... {Isaiah 40:31}

Be strong and take heart and wait upon the lord... {Psalm 27:14}

Sometimes it takes more strength to wait long, than to work hard. Know what I mean?

I think it has something to do with this awful tendency I have to control everything and keep it on my own terms.

Sometimes I want to work, but God wants me to wait.

Early in our marriage, Joey and I had some precious friends who spoke truth and life into our relationship. One of the things they always say of God is this - *He's seldom early, but never late.*

I always remember their words, but I have to keep relearning that lesson.

Saturday was circled on my calendar. I had a speaking engagement that day. I was feeling less prepared than usual because it was a particularly busy time around our house.

Days before I was to take the stage I literally fell to my knees and spent several minutes pleading and crying and asking God to please move me forward in the process. *Please give me direction and focus as I sit down to work on this thing.*

What followed was what felt like two hours of disorganized nothing - wasted time. Forward movement equal to about two inches, when I felt as though I needed two miles.

I was discouraged and uncomfortable and probably pretty difficult to be around {just ask my husband}. That's how well I respond to waiting.

That night I went to bed early and instead of a long diatribe I simply whispered these words to God - *I trust you.*

I think I know why waiting takes more out of me than working.
I try to *work* through the wait. That's when my faith shrinks small and fragile.
I should *trust* through the wait. That's when my faith grows big and strong.

Instead of accepting God's nudging that *now is not the time for you to do that* or *this is not the direction I want you to go with that* - I just keep spinning my wheels figuring I will have to get things moving for him. It's a slippery slope when we try to 'help God out'. Just ask Sarah about that whole episode with Hagar!

I finally submitted. Again – not one of my strong points.

The next morning God flooded me with thoughts and inspiration in the form of an email and an article and the words of a wise friend. Carrying each of those things in my heart, I got into my minivan and drove to the grocery store. During the 15-minute trip my message for the weekend was written and ready. I never even placed my fingers on the keyboard.

Seldom early - never late.

What I released from my hands, God picked right up into his.
What I had spent hours, days, weeks ruminating over, God took and
transformed within a matter of minutes and presented it back to me
- perfectly.

When will I learn that all the hard work I put into my calling is futile
if I have not first been still long enough to wait on the one who has
called me?

~ Pour onto the page everything you have been striving for. What is
consuming all your thoughts, time, and energy right now? Release
those things to God.
~ Now that you have 'emptied', set your timer for 10 minutes and sit
still and silent allowing God to fill you back up with himself. If he
directs you to your Bible – go there. If he doesn't – stay put. If you
feel the need to get on your knees and pray – do it. Whatever you
do, keep releasing and keep waiting.

Today is your fifth 'Finders Keepers'.

{1} Open your Bible {or turn it on}.

{2} Find your verse. You can randomly choose. You can search for a keyword. You can flip to a particular chapter. You can go back to something you were recently intrigued by.

Or choose one from the list below:

~ Hebrews 10:35
~ 1 Corinthians 16:13
~ Romans 14:23
~ John 15:5
~ 2 Chronicles 20:12

Take a breath, allow yourself to be guided to that spot, and then see what you find. This isn't the time to go back to an old favorite. It's time to discover something new.

{3} Read your verse. Read it again. And again. Look at it in various translations. Read 2 or 3 verses surrounding it if you need some context. As you read, don't be too focused on how you can say something profound about the verse, but instead allow the verse to say something profound to you. Even if it's slow going at first, give it some time.

{4} 15 minutes flat. Set your timer. After you've taken a little time to let the words settle into your spirit take 15 minutes to record what you've found. If you have trouble coming up with anything, just copy the verse. Underline words or phrases that resonate with you. Write something about that word or phrase. Remember you are not being graded and there is no 'right' or 'wrong'. Stick to your time limit because if you feel the need to do more you may not do it at all, and that would be a shame.

Come.
Deny yourself.
Follow me.

I am learning what it means to follow Christ.
Not the church, or the pastor, or the crowd,
but Christ.
I am learning how to follow a man—
not a movement.

I am learning how to find Him in a crowd.
How to pick him out.
Recognize his gait,
his gestures,
his profile.
his hair.

He turns,
ever so slightly,
and looks over his shoulder.
Our eyes meet,
his gaze penetrates,
beckoning me onward.
Up and in.
Press on.
Keep up.
Keep going.

I'm coming, Jesus!
I'm coming!

Breathless.
Heart-pounding.
Don't leave me.

Please, don't leave me.
Please.

I am learning how to press through the bodies,
the tightly packed shoulders,
and the bullies who block the way.
I am learning how to press
through them
and into Him.

Just the hem of His garment.
If I could just touch the hem of His garment.[1]

I am learning how to fight,
to wrestle, to struggle--
to persist and persevere,
 to endure—
so I don't fall too far behind.

Don't give up.
Don't get lost.

Even when the brethren melt my heart,[2]
break my back,
bring me to my knees--
I am learning how to rise up,
wounded and weary,
and walk again.

I have decided to follow Jesus
I have decided to follow Jesus
I have decided to follow Jesus
No turning back, no turning back.[3]

---

[1] Matthew 9: 21
[2] Joshua 14: 8, *The Message*
[3] "I Have Decided to Follow Jesus" by S. Sundar Singh

I am learning to pay attention,
to keep my face forward,
eyes open--
on the prize--
so I won't lose him.

I press toward the mark.[4]
Set my face like a flint.

I am learning how to say,
Excuse me, excuse me.
Pardon me. Excuse me.
Again and again,
as I slip past,
squeeze around,
and push aside.

Though none go with me,
still I will follow.
Though none go with me,
still I will follow.
Though none go with me,
still I will follow.
No turning back, no turning back.

I am learning to swim upstream,
against the current.
I am learning to walk the road less travelled,[5]
the narrow way.

I am learning what it is to
move in the wrong direction.
(Right?)

---

[4] Philippians 3: 14
[5] "The Road Not Taken" by Robert Frost

166

Against the flow,
out of step,
out of sync,
dissonant.

I march to the beat of a different drum.

Pa-rum-pa-pum-pum
rum-pa-pum-pum
rum-pa-pum-pum,
me and my drum.[6]

I'm learning (and oh, how it hurts!)
to lay aside the sin that
so easily besets me.
The burden that weighs me down.

I thought I had left my nets.
But here I am again,
tangled in the hemp.

The desires and wishes.
Longings and expectations.
Baubles.
Distractions.
Trifles and trinkets.

I'm learning how to open my hands
and let them all go.
Leave them by the way.
Discarded. Forgotten.

I'll survive without them.
Just give me Jesus.
Living water.

---

[6] "The Little Drummer Boy" by Alex Lifeson

Bread of Life.
Resurrection power.

I am learning to leave all
(or have them leave me--
the nature of the parting is His choosing).
Father and mother,
Houses and lands,
Living and dead.

The world behind me, the cross before me.
The world behind me, the cross before me.
The world behind me, the cross before me.
No turning back,
No turning back.

Oh, friend.
When I get to Him,
get to Jesus--
there may not be much left of me.

I began this journey looking like
I had somewhere to go,
someone to see.
But my lucky outfit is no longer pressed.
It's lost its shape,
and hangs askew.
Miles back my shiny shoes
lost their shimmer.
Scuffed and scraped,
I slipped them off.
Heels blistered.
Soles bleeding.
Hair tangled.
I look a mess.

I've walked through a great wilderness.

I'm not home yet.

God is beckoning me onward—to Jesus,[7]
the Author and Finisher of my faith.[8]
Look to Him!
Run that you may obtain!
Obtain what? What is the prize?

Christ. Christ Himself.
Very God of very God,
begotten not made.[9]
Bone of my bone,
Flesh of my flesh.[10]

Oh, soul! Follow hard!

By the grace and power of God,
Grab hold!

---

[7] Philippians 3, *The Message*
[8] Hebrews 12: 1-2
[9] The Nicene Creed
[10] Genesis 2: 23

Trial and Torture.

Sound like something you would like to read?
How about something you would like to live?

In The Message translation of the Bible this is the heading for the beginning of Chapter 4 of the 2nd letter Paul wrote to the church at Corinth. Paul was familiar with trials and torture in his own life.

Other translations provide contrasting introductions to his words. The ESV titles chapter 4 - *The Light of the Gospel.* That's quite a different sentiment, wouldn't you agree? But I think the NIV pulls it all together - *Present Weakness and Resurrection Life.*

Reading these various descriptions for the same passage of scripture reminds me that we aren't meant to face the trials and tortures of this life without the light of the gospel. And really, our present weakness is directly tied to our resurrection life. This chapter of scripture is a perfect place to begin understanding that truth. God gave it to me during one of the most difficult seasons of my own life.

When both you and your husband wake up on two consecutive nights panic-stricken in a cold sweat feeling like you might need to call 9-1-1 because your heart is trying to pound its way out of your chest it feels a little bit like torture. It is certainly indicative of a trial. Joey was under a tremendous amount of stress at work and we saw some unexpected job changes on the horizon. The conditions were perfect for fear to creep in and do its dirty work.

I've been struck down by fear plenty of times in my life but it is interesting to consider how my fears have changed over the years. But they are still fear. The enemy of my soul is so sneaky that he disguises them in different dark cloaks so I fail to recognize them for a season and allow myself to be tortured before I realize - *oh yeah, this is just that same old fear again - packaged differently.*

Fear is always sourced in this world.
Freedom from fear is always sourced from God.
It's one more reason I must be diligent in shifting my focus from the temporal to the eternal.
From the things that are fleeting to the things that endure.
From the fears this world offers to the freedom of eternity held out to me by the pierced hands of Jesus.

When fear, or any other emotion, has us in a death grip, God has a way of leading us to a specific verse for the specific purpose of setting us free. Here's the one he has given me over and over again to set me free from fear. I want you to hear it three different ways.

Since God has so generously let us in on what he is doing, we're not about to throw up our hands and walk off the job just because we run into occasional hard times.
2 Corinthians 4:1 MSG

Since God, in his mercy, has given us this new way, we never give up.
2 Corinthians 4:1 NLT

Since through God's mercy we have this ministry, we do not lose heart.
2 Corinthians 4:1 NIV

There is so much goodness packed into this little verse. For now, I will say only this.

We all have a ministry.

We all have a job to do - something we were uniquely created to contribute in this world. But the work we do is 'in this world', as Jesus reminded us elsewhere in scripture, will involve trouble, hardship, trials and torture.

We do our ministry in this world, BUT we possess inside of us something of another world - an eternal one. It's why I wanted to make sure you read the final translation from the NIV.

We do not lose heart.

Why? Because guess what has been set in our heart? Eternity.

He has made everything beautiful in its time. He has also set eternity in the human heart; yet no one can fathom what God has done from beginning to end.
Ecclesiastes 3:11

We have a work to do here. Doing work here is hard. Living life here is hard. But it is all still very possible as long as we do not lose heart, do not lose sight of eternity. The good news is this - we don't have to go far to find it.

~ Read the rest of 2 Corinthians 4 and jot down anything significant God offers you during your reading.

Spiritual disciplines help us shift from living life our way to living life God's way. Some may mistakenly think this takes away our freedom, makes us robots, or keeps us from being uniquely ourselves. I hope you will find the opposite to be true. Maybe reading Galatians 5 will help. Take some time to read the entire chapter and highlight or journal about what God's way really looks like. Here is a particularly powerful section of this passage from the Message:

But what happens when we live God's way? He brings gifts into our lives, much the same way that fruit appears in an orchard—things like affection for others, exuberance about life, serenity. We develop a willingness to stick with things, a sense of compassion in the heart, and a conviction that a basic holiness permeates things and people. We find ourselves involved in loyal commitments, not needing to force our way in life, able to marshal and direct our energies wisely.

Legalism is helpless in bringing this about; it only gets in the way. Among those who belong to Christ, everything connected with getting our own way and mindlessly responding to what everyone else calls necessities is killed off for good—crucified.

Since this is the kind of life we have chosen, the life of the Spirit, let us make sure that we do not just hold it as an idea in our heads or a sentiment in our hearts, but work out its implications in every detail of our lives. That means we will not compare ourselves with each other as if one of us were better and another worse. We have far more interesting things to do with our lives. Each of us is an original.
{Galatians 5:22-26}

You are an original. God created you that way. Now that we have *begun*, it's time to *become*. Perhaps another book is around the bend, as we continue to travel this road together.

Lord, teach me to listen.
The times are noisy and my ears are weary
with the thousand raucous sounds
which continuously assault them.
~ A.W. Tozer, "The Pursuit of God"

Epilogue

Nearly every translation of the Bible begins with the exact same words.

In the beginning...

Beginnings are important.

God is the beginning of all things. When we get back to the beginning, we get back to Him. When we are faced with the beginning of a new day, a new job, a new relationship, a new child, a new project, or a new season of life we are wise to always begin the same way – with Him. And not only that, we are wise to remember the two words attached to that very first beginning.

In the beginning, **God created...**

If I were asked to state, as simply as possible, my wish for anyone reading this book I would say this -

Live your God-created life.

Not the life your parents dreamed of.
Not the life you've seen on movie screens.
Not the life of your best friend.
Not the life of that person you follow on Instagram.

It's time to stop playing someone else's song and compose your own. God has a life in mind for you that no one else has ever lived. A song no one else has ever sung. A work of art no one else has ever painted. A story no one else has ever written. Don't miss yours trying to imitate theirs.

No matter how hard we try to 'get things right', there will always be a darkness, a nothingness, a void, unless God is creating something new. Give him the time and space to be your Creator. Something out of nothing is his specialty.

At the beginning of every new day and every new situation in your life, I hope you let God lead. I hope you aren't cowering back in fear or racing ahead in pride. I hope you are confidently acknowledging the presence of your Savior, allowing him to dip his brush into the paints of his sovereignty and grace, covering your life in the colors of his beauty and truth. When that happens you will be a living, breathing display of his glory for all the world to see.

To let God create, you will have to move in close, as often as you can, so he can do his work. His work of art. You.

The Spirit of God lives in you. If you have committed your life to Christ, God had deposited his Spirit inside of you. This is why disciplines of the Spirit are so important. If we spend all of our time focused on everything 'out there' demanding our attention we will fail to be attuned to the what is 'in here' seeking to guide us and care for us.

Recognizing God's presence, hearing from him, learning from him, being led by him, can only happen when we abstain from the things 'out there' and engage in the things 'in here' – in his word, in his presence, and in our very own being. If someone dares to tell you all this 'begin business' is making you self-absorbed, smile and ignore them. There is much we carry within ourselves that must be absorbed.

The closer you get to God, the more obedient you must be. Some choose the level of obedience whereby they endeavor to avoid sin and choose righteousness. That was the level where the children of

Israel, who knew God's <u>acts</u>, lived. Moses, however, knew God's <u>ways</u>. The issue for Moses was no longer simply, "Is this action right or wrong?" The issue was, "What is God's command?"
~ Bob Sorge, *Secrets of the Secret Place*

The world is full of opinions about right and wrong, good and bad. We get hung up on semantics or situational exceptions and fail to come to an agreement on many things.

There is a better question.
What is God's best?

That is the same thing as saying,
What is God's command?

His commands are always pointing towards what is best. God's best takes into account the sum total of all the yesterdays, todays, and tomorrows. For that reason, what may appear best to us may very well be the thing God knows he must spare us from today because of what it might mean tomorrow.

What does God say for <u>me</u> to do on <u>this</u> day, in <u>this</u> particular situation to bring about <u>His</u> desired result? That is the question. That is the path of obedience which leads into open fields of freedom.

What God says and does is truth. He *is* truth and therefore all truth comes from Him. To know Him, is to know truth.

Apart from him I can do nothing.
~Jesus

If it was true for Jesus, it is most certainly true for us.

When we consider Jesus as a historical figure, we study and seek to understand his *acts*. When we consider Jesus a personal friend, we experience and seek to understand his *ways*. There is a vast difference. It is the difference in a life of bearing eternal fruit and a life that will eventually shrivel up and die.

If God speaks to us at all other than through such official channels as the Bible and the church, then I think he speaks to us largely through what happens to us. If we keep our hearts and minds open as well as our ears, if we listen with patience and hope, if we remember at all deeply and honestly, then I think we come to recognize, beyond all doubt, that, however faintly we may hear him, he is indeed speaking to us, and that, however little we may understand of it, his word to each of us is both recoverable and precious beyond telling.
Frederick Buechner

Remember Oliver at the piano?
In position.
Eyes closed.
Listening.
Creating.
Calling it 'good'.

In the beginning of all beginnings, God created and called it 'good' too. He's still doing it today. Getting in the presence of your Creator will not require you to take a long and arduous journey. You're already there. He's already here.

Listen.
Close your eyes.
You're in position, in His presence.

~~~

It is difficult to end a book about beginnings. As we say goodbye, promise me you will always remember...
beginnings never end.

Always we begin again.

About the Contributors

Look at all these beautiful faces!
Oh how I wish we could gather together with you on the back porch for a visit. Below you will discover a little bit about each of my friends who contributed to *begin*. These are their own words, and here's what I find fascinating about them. When I asked for a short bio, I expected them to include some of the projects they are working on, books they have written, organizations they have led, and offices they have held. Not a single one of them did that. They all talked about who they are independent of their earthly accomplishments {and, trust me, those accomplishments are many!}. This is what it means to have a healthy identity in Christ. We don't need to brag or boast, we just need to be the women God has created us to be! If you're looking for some new friends, I highly recommend them. Connect on Instagram or their websites.

KARINA ALLEN is devoted to helping women live out their calling and building authentic community through practical application of scripture in an approachable, winsome manner.

IG: @karina268
forhisnameandhisrenown.
wordpress.com

LEIGH ANDERSON is wife to Brian, mom of two toddlers, and a ministry leader in her local church. Her top passions are her family and pouring into the hearts of young moms. Leigh uses the tool of personal transparency and vulnerability, no matter how bad it makes her look, to show moms they aren't alone.

IG: @theleighanderson

HALEY BARINOWSKI is a shameless Clemson fanatic who survives on dessert and throwing football. She loves good books, good pens, and good runs.

IG: @haleybarinowski
haleybarinowski.wordpress.com

AMY BENNETT is wife to her high school sweetheart and mom to their 3 children. She writes programming code for a bank by day and faith-filled words for her blog by night.

IG: @bennettaj
amyjbennett.com

AMANDA DILDAY is a weary warrior, being made new—as a wife, mother, writer, & teacher. She is friend of the plants, student of the stars, and seeker of Truth. She is learning what it means to be a precious and beloved daughter of God.

alchemillas.com

BREANN NICHOLSON has a passion for Jesus, being a wife, serving others and making art through storytelling.

IG: @thebreannnicholson
lifeasanicholson.wordpress.com

KAI PINEDA is wife to a pastor, mom to a Maltipoo named McLovin, and a serious Jesus Girl who loves communicating the Gospel.

IG: @kai_a_pineda
kaipineda.com

BETH PLYLER is wife to the love of her life, mom to three little crazy people and one human-like Weimaraner. She's a counselor, lover of dark chocolate, almonds and red wine. She stays up too late and travels to Clemson or Kiawah Island every chance she gets.

given-goods.com

ELIZABETH POPLIN is married to her college sweetheart and Mommy to her wish-come-true boys. She is a Bible teacher and writer, teaching women they are earnestly treasured, perfectly loved, and relentlessly pursued by a matchless God. Elizabeth lives in North Carolina with lots of Legos, laundry, and love.

IG: @awakencharlotte

MINDY RODENBURG is a transplanted Southerner with a heart for purposeful connection in home + business + life

IG: @mindyrodenburg
mindyrodenburg.com

TERESA SWANSTROM ANDERSON is a busy mama of six (four from Ethiopia), a writer, speaker, and blogger. She loves setting a beautiful table, is passionate about celebrating the everyday, and believes in instilling the love of God into her children's hearts and the hearts of women everywhere.

IG: @teresaswanstromanderson
teresaswanstromanderson.com

AMANDA UHER is a wife, mom, & writer who loves Jesus and the adventure of walking with Him (even when she trips and falls on her face).

IG: @amandauher
amandauher.com

About the Author

ELIZABETH MAXON is a storyteller, truth seeker, beauty beholder, grace giver, and word weaver.

She is wife to a handsome golf coach named Joey, and mama to her wild monkeys, Lucy and Oliver. She routinely chooses to read a book rather than put away laundry and visit with friends rather than do the grocery shopping. This makes her a terrible housekeeper and an average cook, but her people love her anyway. Together they live on the edge of the woods in the little college town of Clemson, South Carolina.

Elizabeth has also written
Onederland: A Mother's Story of Finding Hope in the Hard Places

Connect with her at elizabethmaxon.com or on IG @elizabethmaxon

Final Note

But the Helper, the Holy Spirit, whom the Father will send in my name, he will teach you all things and bring to your remembrance all that I have said to you.
{John 14:26}

Remembering is important.

At the end of each leg of our journey we are wise to turn around and spend a few moments looking back. If my prayers have been answered, God has spoken to you over the last weeks and months. He has brought change into your heart and your life. You are not the same person you were on page one. Neither am I.

Before you move on to the next leg of your journey, *remember.*

Look back over the phrases you underlined and the notes you made in the margins. Pull out your journal and find the common threads woven there. What has God done? And where is He leading you next?

Please share your journey with us by using the hastag #beginbook or emailing me at elizabethmaxoninc@gmail.com

ELIZABETH MAXON

one derland

a mother's story of
FINDING HOPE IN THE HARD PLACES

Sometimes our greatest struggles
set the stage for a greater story.

For more information: www.elizabethmaxon.com
#typeonederland